D0463109

Hate
Crimes

by Michael V. Uschan

LUCENT BOOKS

An imprint of Thomson Gale, a part of The Thomson Corporation

Detroit • New York • San Francisco • New Haven, Conn. • Waterville, Maine • London

THOMSON
GALE
™

© 2007 Thomson Gale, a part of The Thomson Corporation.

Thomson and Star Logo are trademarks and Gale and Lucent Books are registered trademarks used herein under license.

For more information, contact
Lucent Books
27500 Drake Rd.
Farmington Hills, MI 48331-3535
Or you can visit our Internet site at http://www.gale.com

LIBRARY OF CONGRESS CATALOGING-IN-PUBLICATION DATA

Uschan, Michael V., 1948-
  Hate crimes / by Michael V. Uschan.
    p. cm. — (Hot topics)
  Includes bibliographical references and index.
  ISBN 978-1-56006-661-3 (hardcover)
  1. Hate crimes—Juvenile literature. I. Title.
  HV6773.5.U73 2007
  364.15—dc22

                                                          2007007791

ISBN-10: 1-56006-661-X

Printed in the United States of America

CONTENTS

FOREWORD

Young people today are bombarded with information. Aside from traditional sources such as newspapers, television, and the radio, they are inundated with a nearly continuous stream of data from electronic media. They send and receive e-mails and instant messages, read and write online "blogs," participate in chat rooms and forums, and surf the Web for hours. This trend is likely to continue. As Patricia Senn Breivik, the dean of university libraries at Wayne State University in Detroit, states, "Information overload will only increase in the future. By 2020, for example, the available body of information is expected to double every 73 days! How will these students find the information they need in this coming tidal wave of information?"

Ironically, this overabundance of information can actually impede efforts to understand complex issues. Whether the topic is abortion, the death penalty, gay rights, or obesity, the deluge of fact and opinion that floods the print and electronic media is overwhelming. The news media report the results of polls and studies that contradict one another. Cable news shows, talk radio programs, and newspaper editorials promote narrow viewpoints and omit facts that challenge their own political biases. The World Wide Web is an electronic minefield where legitimate scholars compete with the postings of ordinary citizens who may or may not be well-informed or capable of reasoned argument. At times, strongly worded testimonials and opinion pieces both in print and electronic media are presented as factual accounts.

Conflicting quotes and statistics can confuse even the most diligent researchers. A good example of this is the question of whether or not the death penalty deters crime. For instance, one study found that murders decreased by nearly one-third when the death penalty was reinstated in New York in 1995. Death penalty supporters cite this finding to support their argument that the existence of the death penalty deters criminals from committing murder. However, another study found that states without the death penalty have murder rates below the national average. This study is cited by opponents of capital punishment, who reject the claim that the death penalty deters murder. Students need context and clear, informed discussion if they are to think critically and make informed decisions.

The Hot Topics series is designed to help young people wade through the glut of fact, opinion, and rhetoric so that they can think critically about controversial issues. Only by reading and thinking critically will they be able to formulate a viewpoint that is not simply the parroted views of others. Each volume of the series focuses on one of today's most pressing social issues and provides a balanced overview of the topic. Carefully crafted narrative, fully documented primary and secondary source quotes, informative sidebars, and study questions all provide excellent starting points for research and discussion. Full-color photographs and charts enhance all volumes in the series. With its many useful features, the Hot Topics series is a valuable resource for young people struggling to understand the pressing issues of the modern era.

INTRODUCTION

THE SCOPE OF HATE CRIMES

Thousands of hate crimes are committed each year in the United States. These criminal acts occur in every state, and their victims include men, women, and children of all ages and from all walks of life. The hate crimes listed below are typical of those that occur daily across the nation, and they all happened in the span of a few weeks in 2006:

- On June 10 musician Kevin Aviance, whose hit songs "Alive" and "Din Da Da" have topped the Billboard dance chart, was brutally beaten after he left the Phoenix, a popular gay bar in Manhattan, New York. Four men shouted antigay slurs at Aviance, who dresses as a woman when he performs, and then proceeded to kick and beat him with bottles and spray-paint cans. Aviance was hospitalized with injuries that included a broken jaw; the four assailants were later arrested.

- One day later, four white teenagers attacked and robbed two Mexican immigrants who were fishing on a beach in Rocky Point, New York. As they beat their victims, the teens screamed racial and ethnic slurs and ranted that illegal immigrants were taking jobs that only U.S. citizens deserved.

- During the early morning hours of June 30, unknown vandals spray-painted Nazi swastikas and racial slurs on the FiveSix Ultra Lounge in Green Bay, Wisconsin. The bar is owned by Green Bay Packers linebacker Nick Barnett, who is black. He named the bar after his uniform number—56.

- On July 3 in Lewiston, Maine, a man threw a pig's head into the Lewiston-Auburn Islamic Center while Muslims were praying. Muslims consider pigs to be unclean creatures. They were deeply offended because they believed the animal carcass had defiled their place of worship.

Musician Kevin Aviance was brutally beaten by four men in June 2006 because he is gay.

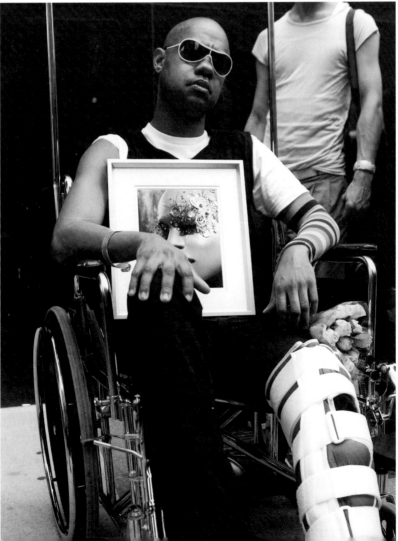

The criminal offenses in these incidents include vandalism, assault, and robbery. However, these acts also belong to another category of unlawful conduct: They are all hate crimes.

What Is a Hate Crime?

People began to use the term *hate crime* to refer to such offenses in the late 1980s following the death of twenty-three-year-old Michael Griffith, an African American. Griffith was walking through Howard Beach, New York, on December 20, 1986, when three whites attacked him because they did not want blacks in their neighborhood. After beating Griffith, the whites chased him. Griffith was so terrified and wanted to get away from his tormentors so badly that he ran onto a busy highway. He died when a car struck him.

Griffith's death and other hate-related incidents created a growing awareness about this problem and led Congress to pass the Hate Crime Statistics Act in April 1990. Annually since 1992 the Federal Bureau of Investigation (FBI) has collected and published data on hate crimes to keep law enforcement officials and the public aware of the problem. The FBI compiles the statistics with the help of state and local law enforcement officials. In *Hate Crime Statistics 2005*, the FBI listed 7,163 hate-crime incidents. These crimes involved 8,380 separate criminal offenses, 6,804 perpetrators, and 8,804 victims. The FBI defines hate crimes as

> criminal offenses that are motivated, in whole or in part, by the offender's bias against [the victim]. In its broadest sense, the term refers to an attack on an individual or his or her property (e.g., vandalism, arson, assault, murder) in which the victim is intentionally selected because of his or her race, color, religion, national origin, gender, disability, or sexual orientation.[1]

A hate crime is any criminal offense in which bias—prejudice against or hatred of an individual based on criteria such as race or sexual orientation—is the reason the perpetrator committed the act. The statistics categorize hate crimes according to the bias that motivated them. These categories include race, religion, sexual orientation (whether someone is gay, lesbian, bisexual, or transgender), ethnic background or national origin, and physical and mental disabilities.

All of the 2006 incidents listed above can be considered hate crimes under this definition. Kevin Aviance was targeted because of his sexual orientation, the two Mexican immigrants because of their ethnicity, Nick Barnett for his race, and the Muslims for their religion. In the June 11 hate crime in Rocky Point, New York, police sergeant Robert Reecks said the two immigrants had done nothing to provoke the brutal beating: "These men were just sitting on the jetty, minding their own business."[2] The whites attacked them because they disliked Latinos, an attitude they displayed by shouting racial and ethnic slurs while they beat the two men.

Hate: The Root of Evil

The offenses that constitute hate crimes are endless. They range from relatively harmless acts like spray-painting offensive graffiti

Pakistani Rashid Alam, lying in bed, was beaten by a mob of white men. This is considered a hate crime because the men were motivated to beat Alam only because of his ethnic background.

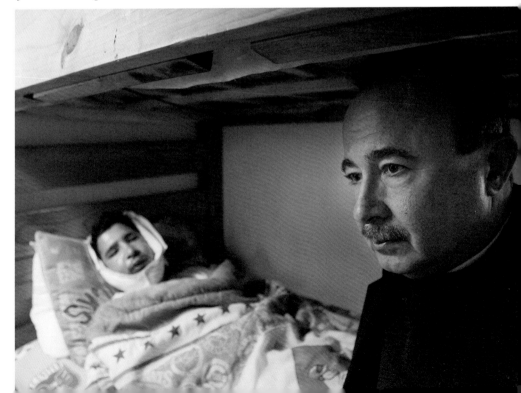

The Holocaust, in which the Nazis murdered millions of Jews and others thought to be inferior, is one of history's most heinous and wide-reaching hate crimes.

on buildings to violent acts such as arson, assault, rape, and murder. No matter what type of conduct is involved, hate crimes are triggered by the same factor—hatred of the victims because they are different in some way from the perpetrator.

One of history's greatest hate crimes occurred during World War II when Nazi Germany systematically murdered 11 million people in the Holocaust. The Nazis built death camps in which they killed many types of people whom they considered inferior because they were different: Jews, Gypsies, Slavic people from Poland and Russia, homosexuals, and the mentally and physically disabled. Elie Wiesel, a Jew, survived Nazi death camps to track down and bring to justice many Nazis who led the Holocaust. He once said that hatred of people who are different is such a powerful force that it allows people to commit the worst crimes imaginable: "Hatred is at the root of evil everywhere. Racial hatred, ethnic hatred, political hatred, religious hatred. In its name, all seems permitted. For those who glorify hatred [the] end justifies all means, including the most despicable ones."[3]

HOW PEOPLE LEARN TO HATE

On July 17, 2006, twenty-year-old Nicholas Minucci was sentenced to fifteen years in prison for using a baseball bat to fracture the skull of twenty-three-year-old Glenn Moore. Minucci had been convicted of robbery and assault as a hate crime against Moore, an African American. Minucci attacked Moore on June 29, 2005, because he did not want blacks in his predominantly white Howard Beach, New York, neighborhood. The incident was eerily similar to the Howard Beach slaying two decades earlier of Michael Griffith, a racial assault that helped draw national attention to the growing problem of hate crimes. When Queens Supreme Court justice Richard Buchter sentenced Minucci, he condemned Minucci for his hatred of blacks, which he had displayed by shouting racial slurs as he was beating

Hate crime perpetrators, such as Nicholas Minucci, pictured, who received fifteen years in prison for beating a black man, are motivated to hurt others simply because they are different from themselves.

Moore. "What has caused more sadness and suffering in this nation than racism?" asked Buchter. "The defendant's words and actions and the very nature of the crime send out a deplorable message of intolerance."[4]

This was the second hate crime Minucci had committed. A few days after the Muslim terrorist group al Qaeda attacked New York City and Washington, D.C., on September 11, 2001, Minucci had been arrested for shooting paintballs at two men who were wearing turbans. Minucci had thought they were Muslims, but they were actually Sikhs—members of an East Indian religion—who had been on their way to pray for victims of the terrorist attack. Minucci had been placed on probation for that incident.

SOCIALIZED TO HATE?

"Children are socialized to hate [people who are different] in exactly the same way they are socialized to accept other conceptions of what should be valued, such as motherhood, patriotism, and personal success."

Jack Levin and Gordana Rabrenovic, *Why We Hate.* Amherst, NY: Prometheus, 2004, p. 69.

The link between both of Minucci's hate crimes was the fact that his victims were different from him in either skin color or the way they looked. Physically assaulting someone because he or she is different is a crime. However, noting such differences in other people is something that everyone does every day.

"Us" and "Them"

When humans see or meet other people for the first time, they note facts about them such as their age, race, how they dress, and how they speak. Sara Bullard, a sociologist and expert on how to be tolerant of other people, explains that making such comparisons is a natural part of human nature: "The first thing we do when we notice strangers is to notice the ways they are like us or different from us." She states that humans do this in an attempt to understand other people in relationship to themselves. Humans generally feel more comfortable with people who are similar to them. Bullard says, "We gravitate toward those who are like us. We are apparently born with a tendency to prefer the familiar and withdraw from the unfamiliar."[5]

For example, when people get on a bus, they prefer to sit next to someone they know rather than a stranger. If they do not know anyone, they will look to share a seat with someone who is like them in some way—young or old, white or black, male or female. People prefer to sit next to someone who shares a familiar characteristic with them because it makes that person seem less like a stranger. Sociologists and psychologists claim that most people are cautious about strangers due to a fear that goes back to humankind's primitive ancestors.

In *Why We Hate*, authors Jack Levin and Gordana Rabrenovic explain that thousands of years ago primitive people feared anyone who was not a member of their immediate group, whether that unit was a family or a tribe: "The survival of early humankind depended in part on being wary of strangers. Until and unless they were proven otherwise, outsiders were considered the enemy."[6] Levin and Rabrenovic say this fear helped primitive people survive because strangers did sometimes attack them, steal their food, seize their land, or kill them. Primitive people recognized strangers

Noticing the ways in which someone is different from you is a natural human reaction. To hurt someone because of that difference is a hate crime.

by the ways in which they were different, whether it was their physical features, language, or clothing.

Along with other psychologists and sociologists, Levin and Rabrenovic believe that most humans today still instinctively fear people who are different. They claim that this trait has been passed down to modern men and women both genetically and through learned behavior instilled in them from generation to generation. Psychologist Ervin Staub believes this fear of strangers has an important effect on human relations. He argues that mentally dividing people into two categories—those who are similar and those who are not—is a key step toward hating people who are different: "Hate is rooted in and develops from the human tendency to differentiate between *us* and *them* and the many ways that people come to devalue [think negatively about] *them*. The line be-

Even Animals Reject Strangers

As author Sara Bullard writes in her book *Teaching Tolerance,* scientists believe that one of the traits humans have inherited from their animal ancestors is the tendency to reject members of their species who are different. This is true of chimpanzees, a primate closely related to humans through evolution:

> Chimpanzees are famously friendly among their own groups, but they "simply can't stand the sight of strangers," observed [scientist] Carl Sagan in his book *Shadows of Forgotten Ancestors.* Unfamiliar chimps provoke immediate outrage. They are routinely attacked and killed. In 1966, Jane Goodall was watching

when a polio epidemic struck a group of chimps at Gombe Reservation in Tanzania, leaving several chimps partially paralyzed. Goodall wrote: "Crippled by their disease, they were forced to move in odd ways, dragging limbs. Other chimps were at first afraid; then they threatened the afflicted, and then attacked them." The insistence on the dominance of "our" group and the antagonism toward strangers is very common among animals.

Sara Bullard, *Teaching Tolerance: Raising Open-Minded, Empathetic Children.* New York: Doubleday, 1996, p. 28.

tween *us* and *them* can be drawn on many bases, and it can be arbitrarily and easily created."[7] And the differences that humans use to assign other people to such groups are almost limitless. They range from race or religion to the school the other person attends and even the sports team they support.

Stereotypes and Hatred

When humans divide their world into "us" and "them," they no longer recognize members of "them" groups as individuals but only as units of a group. This is important because humans have a different method of relating to people they have assigned to a group than to people they meet and judge on an individual basis.

Psychologists Robert M. Baird and Stuart E. Rosenbaum claim that humans usually rely on stereotypes—prejudgments of entire groups of people—to guide their actions toward people they consider different. Baird and Rosenbaum claim that people like to apply stereotypes about groups to all their members because it is faster and easier than assessing each person on an individual basis: "We humans have a need to simplify our interactions with others into efficient patterns. This essential simplification leads naturally to stereotyping as a means to the desired efficiency."[8]

Stereotypes make it easier to understand people, but there are many problems in using them to categorize people. One problem is that members of any group all have their own individual strengths and weaknesses. Secondly, stereotypes are often false because they are based on limited contact with such people; many white people who hate blacks, for example, rarely have much social contact with them. The third problem is that group stereotypes are almost always negative.

Gordon W. Allport, a psychologist who pioneered key theories about hatred, claimed that people willingly accept such negative stereotypes because of a basic human need to feel superior to other people. Allport wrote, "The easiest idea to sell anyone is that he is better than someone else."[9] Thus, whites are eager to believe that they are inherently smarter than blacks, people born in the United States that they are superior to natives of other countries, or members of any religion that their faith is the only true one. Yet people are not born believing stereotypes and scorning those who are different. Instead, they must learn such prejudices before they can begin hating other people.

Taught to Hate?

A prejudice is a preconceived negative attitude toward members of a particular group that is not based on facts. Prejudices can be learned from many sources. Three main influences on the ideas and attitudes that people acquire about their world while they are growing up, including prejudices, are their families, the culture of the community in which they live, and the mass media.

A person's family is an especially powerful influence. From the day children are born, parents and other relatives teach them a multitude of lessons about values, priorities, and attitudes. One of the most important lessons children learn from their parents is how to act toward other people. For example, if a child's parents hate blacks, that boy or girl is likely to adopt similar racist feelings. Clinton Sipes is a white supremacist who spent time in prison for hate crimes but

Children are not born with hate; it is learned. Family can greatly influence how a young person develops his or her attitudes toward people who are different from them.

Learning to Hate

In their book *Hate Crimes Revisited,* sociologists Jack Levin and Jack McDevitt discuss how people learn to hate others:

> Learning to hate is almost as inescapable as breathing. Like almost everyone else, the hate crime offender grows up in a culture that defines certain people as righteous, upstanding citizens, while designating others as sleazy, immoral characters who deserve to be mistreated. As a child, the perpetrator may never have had a firsthand experience with members of the groups he later comes to despise and then victimize. But, early on, merely by conversing with his family, friends, and teachers or by watching his favorite television programs, he learns the characteristics of disparaging stereotypes. He also learns that it is socially acceptable, perhaps even expected, to repeat racist jokes and use ethnic slurs and epithets. Columnist Walter Lippmann long ago coined the term "stereotype" in references to the "pictures in our heads"—the generalizations that we have concerning different groups of people. All the members of Group W are "terrorists who hate Americans." All the members of Group X are "dirty" and "lazy." All the members of Group Y are "money hungry," "powerful," and "shrewd." All the members of Group Z are "sexual predators."

Jack Levin and Jack McDevitt, *Hate Crimes Revisited: America's War Against Those Who Are Different.* Cambridge, MA: Westview, 2002, p. 27.

later rejected his hatred of blacks. He says his racism was shaped by his parents' attitudes: "The house I grew up in, when [civil rights leader] Martin Luther King, Jr., was mentioned on TV, it was 'There's that agitator, that problem-maker.' All I ever heard was bad things about Martin Luther King."[10] The negative comments about King that Sipes heard led him to believe that all blacks were bad. This attitude disposed him to dislike blacks even before he met them.

Children can also be influenced by cultural attitudes held by the people in the community, state, and region in which they live. Children learn from comments they hear daily from friends, neighbors, and other people. If people whom children respect make negative statements about blacks, gays, or immigrants, or they treat them with disrespect, children will tend to adopt similar attitudes toward such people. This is especially true if the person making the negative comment is an authority figure like a teacher, church or community leader, or elected official.

Gregory M. Herek is a professor of psychology at the University of California, Davis. He believes a major factor in the slaying of Matthew Shepard on October 6, 1998, was that so many people in Wyoming hated gays that it was culturally acceptable to do so. After meeting Shepard in a bar in Laramie, Russell Henderson and Aaron McKinney robbed and beat the University of Wyoming student. They then tied Shepard to a fence and left him to die. Herek claims the two men thought their actions were justified by antigay sentiments they had heard throughout their lives:

> The killers most certainly had a lifelong exposure to society's messages about how men and women should behave and how homosexuals should be regarded. They may have believed that no one would mind the loss of another homosexual. [Such] attacks can persist only

The suspects in the Matthew Shepard murder, sitting in front, grew up in a culture that tolerated hatred of homosexuals.

when society defines itself in terms of "us" and "them," and systematically deprives "them" of their humanity.[11]

The mass media also shape attitudes about people who are different. Newspaper, magazine, and Internet stories about gays, Latinos, and Muslims influence how people feel about them. For example, news articles about high crime levels in black neighborhoods may make readers feel that all blacks are criminals even though that is not true. Television shows and films sometimes lend believability to stereotypes by using them to portray fictional characters.

GROWING UP WITH PREJUDICE

"By the time most children are big enough to ride a bicycle, they know who the outsiders are and they know what to call them: jerk, fatso, nerd. . . . No one had to explain these things. It's one of the inevitable lessons of being alive in America."

Sara Bullard, *Teaching Tolerance: Raising Open-Minded, Empathetic Children.* New York: Doubleday, 1996, p. 8.

Even popular music can help stereotypes gain acceptance. The rap group Public Enemy has been criticized for anti-Semitic lyrics in its songs. Richard Griffin, a group member known as Professor Griff, once used an anti-Jewish stereotype in a news conference when he claimed that "Jews are wicked. They create wickedness around the globe."[12] Likewise, white rapper Eminem (Marshall Mathers) openly sings antigay lyrics. Although these and other artists are publicly criticized for their racist comments and prejudicial lyrics, their popularity is hardly diminished by such controversy. Entertainers such as Public Enemy and Eminem have huge fan bases, so the stereotypes they propagate reach listeners around the world, influencing the beliefs of devoted fans. Yet such comments and song lyrics are more than mere entertainment; they are classified as hate speech. Hate speech is one of several factors that can trigger people to commit hate crimes.

From Hate Speech to Hate Crimes

The term *hate speech* refers to any form of expression designed to hurt or belittle members of a particular group. It includes derogatory

The antigay lyrics sung by rap star Eminem send the wrong message to his listeners: that hating gays is acceptable.

comments printed on leaflets, graffiti in the form of racist slogans or symbols painted on buildings, and symbolic acts such as burning a cross, a traditional Ku Klux Klan tactic to frighten blacks. Most hate speech is legal in the United States because the First Amendment to the Constitution guarantees freedom of speech.

During a 2001 debate in Texas regarding a hate-crime bill, state representative Senfronia Thompson, an African American, explained the dividing line that separates the two forms of hate: "You want to call me all kinds of names? Call me a no-good, low-down, dirty nigger? Help yourself. But the minute you hit me, you better look out, because it becomes something else."[13] Thompson knows that a punch, unlike a racial epithet, is a hate crime.

Hate speech can also incite people to commit hate crimes. That may have been the case with Benjamin Nathaniel Smith. During the 1999 Fourth of July weekend, Smith killed two people and wounded nine more in a three-day shooting spree motivated by his hatred of blacks, Asians, and Jews. The hate rampage ended when Smith shot himself to death after being surrounded by law enforcement officers. Several months earlier, Smith had explained in an interview for a documentary film how Internet sites had helped him clarify his views toward such people. According to Smith, "It wasn't really 'til I got on the Internet, read some literature of these groups that [his hate-filled ideas] really all came together. It's a slow, gradual process to become racially conscious."[14] Reading such hateful ideas strengthened Smith's racism and compelled him to embark on a murderous rampage.

A VICIOUS CYCLE

"Hate crimes directed at individuals with disabilities are perhaps the most insidious of all unlawful behaviors. Even a single hate crime reminds us that ignorance begets negative attitudes that beget prejudice that begets hatred that begets violence."

Brian T. McMahon et al., "Hate Crimes and Disability in America," *Rehabilitation Counseling Bulletin*, 2004, p. 768.

In addition to hate speech, specific events or situations can also trigger hate crimes. The September 11, 2001, terrorist attack on the United States by the Muslim group al Qaeda led to many hate crimes against Muslims. Increased tension over illegal Mexican immigration in 2005 and 2006 ignited a wave of ethnic hate crimes against Latinos. Hate-crime experts claim that most of the people who committed such offenses already hated Muslims and Latinos and were only using those issues as an excuse to harm them. Mark Potok edits a magazine for the Southern Poverty Law Center (SPLC), which fights hate crime. On May 17, 2006, Potok said hate groups were using the illegal immigration issue to make people angry enough to physically assault Latinos and to deny Latinos their rights: "They're trying to generate a hostile social climate that fosters bigotry and violence towards all Hispanics, whether they're in the country illegally or not."[15]

The Victim Is Not Human

Although many people hate others for being different, very few of the haters commit hate crimes. Sociologists Jack Levin and Jack McDevitt claim that most people who commit hate crimes have something in common: a belief that their victims are so inferior to them that they cannot be considered human beings. This belief makes perpetrators feel it is all right to do things to their victims

Hate crime laws, such as the James Byrd Jr. Hate Crimes Act in Texas, shown being signed into law in 2001, punish the perpetrators of such crimes.

that they would never think about doing to someone they considered human, including beating and even murdering them. Levin and McDevitt say:

> If he [the perpetrator] views the target of his attack as a flesh-and-blood human being with feelings, friends, and a family, the offender may feel guilty. By accepting a dehumanized image of the victim, however, the perpetrator may actually come to believe that his crime was justified. After all, the rules of civilized society apply only to human beings, not to demons or animals.[16]

HATE CRIMES BASED ON RACE

In January 2001 three white teenagers videotaped themselves as they drove through Anchorage, Alaska, while firing paintball guns at Native Alaskans. The video was horrifying for the hatred that it displayed. "We're going to nail some Eskimos," one teenager said in the videotape of the racist spree. After they were arrested and the tape was made public, the *Anchorage Daily News* said the attack was only one of many hate crimes that whites regularly commit against the forty-ninth state's original inhabitants:

> The brutality of these particular teenagers is of a piece, psychologically, with uncounted incidents in our community ranging from the rape and murder of Native women to the all too common stereotyping of "drunk Natives" as somehow subhuman and deserving of whatever attacks they suffer. The level of violence varies from incident to incident, but the common elements are racial bigotry and the dehumanization of others.[17]

The editorial summed up how some people justify committing racial hate crimes. The racist whites somehow believed their victims were inferior just because they were Native Alaskan.

Hate Crimes Caused by Racism

In *Hate Crime Statistics 2005*, the Federal Bureau of Investigation listed racial bias as the cause of 4,691 of the nation's 8,380 hate crimes. A total of 3,200 hate crimes against blacks accounted for well over half of all such offenses; 935 crimes were against whites, 231 were against Asians and Pacific Islanders, 95 were against American Indians and Alaskan Natives, and 230 involved people of multiple races.

Statistics fail to convey the human toll of hate crimes in which offenders defaced buildings and homes with racist graffiti, taunted individuals with racial slurs, and beat up and killed people. In 2003 white college students attacked Jeff Woo and four Chinese friends in San Francisco, California. Woo was knocked to the ground by a punch and was then kicked repeatedly by students shouting racial slurs. Woo says he and his friends were hurt by the fact that they were attacked because of their race. "Hatred just because we're Chinese is pretty messed up,"[18] he says.

The attack on Woo was motivated by a particular form of hatred—racism. In *White Supremacy*, George Frederickson explains that for some people, the physical, cultural, and social differences that they have learned to hate can be attributed to a person's race: "Racists make the claim that such differences are due mainly to immutable genetic factors."[19] In U.S. history, no group has suffered more from racial hatred than African Americans.

Slavery and the Lynching of Blacks

In 1619 the first twenty blacks who arrived in the English colony that would one day become the state of Virginia were sold as slaves. For the next two centuries, African Americans were bought

As recently as the 1960s, many areas of the United States had separate facilities— such as drinking fountains, waiting rooms, and restrooms—for blacks, also called "colored people," and whites.

and sold as property. They had no rights and were whipped for minor offenses like talking back to their white masters, brutal treatment that today would be considered a hate crime.

In the United States, slavery did not end until 1865, when the North defeated the South in the Civil War. Yet the abolition of this cruel practice did not end mistreatment of blacks. White racists immediately began a campaign of violence to keep African Americans politically and socially powerless. Acting individually or in groups like the Ku Klux Klan (KKK), whites beat, raped, and murdered blacks. Whites did this to make blacks so afraid that they would always accept whatever whites did to them. This included forcing blacks to endure segregation, a legal and social system that reduced blacks to second-class citizens by denying them civil rights such as being able to vote.

SCHOOLYARD TAUNTS

"At age ten [in 1985], I immigrated from China to Oakland, California. In elementary school my name soon became 'Ching Chong,' 'Chinagirl,' and 'Chow Mein.' Other children laughed at my language, my culture, my ethnicity, and my race."

Ying Ma, "Black Racism," *American Enterprise,* November/December 1998, p. 54.

A favorite fear tactic whites used against blacks was lynching. This term originally meant putting a criminal to death without due process of law, but after the Civil War it became synonymous with organized brutality against blacks. Between 1882 and 1968, when the last officially documented lynching occurred, whites killed 3,445 black men, women, and children by hanging, shooting, burning, stabbing, and torturing them. The violence continued unchecked until the 1960s, when federal, state, and local governments finally began protecting blacks. But even today blacks are not safe from racism.

Blacks Still Face Racial Hatred

Some people continue to express racist ideas. They distribute literature and operate Web sites that demean blacks, record racist songs, and burn crosses, a traditional KKK symbol of racial hatred.

The Ku Klux Klan (KKK) continues to spread its message of hate in the twenty-first century.

One of the most common hate crimes against blacks is to paint racist graffiti on homes and buildings. On the evening of July 8, 2006, someone spray-painted a red swastika across the garage door of a home in Lake Elsinore, California, that was owned by Nannette Simmons, who is black. Simmons says, "If someone was trying to scare us it didn't work—we're not easily intimidated."[20] Simmons's home was also defaced with the Nazi symbol in 1995, when she first came to the predominantly white community. It is believed that blacks moving into previously white neighborhoods ignite almost half of all racially inspired hate crimes.

Racial hatred also still sparks violence. On June 7, 1998, forty-nine-year-old James Byrd Jr. was murdered in Jasper, Texas. Byrd was chained to a pickup truck and was dragged for 3 miles (4.8km). When Jasper County sheriff Billy Rowles questioned Shawn Allen Berry, one of three white men whom witnesses claimed they had seen with Byrd the night he died, he confessed that they had attacked Byrd because he was African American. The attack on Byrd by Shawn Allen Berry, John William King, and Lawrence Russell Brewer was not motivated by an argument or disagreement between Byrd and the white men; it was not motivated by theft or any other typical reason for a crime. Berry and the other two men attacked Byrd simply because of his hatred for African Americans. Rowles was shocked at the hatred for blacks that Berry expressed in his confession, which was laced with racial slurs: "That just echoed in my head. That's when we realized what we had [was a hate crime]."[21] Byrd remained alive through most of the attack, and the brutal slaying was considered one of the most vicious hate crimes that had occurred in decades.

Race was also the motivating factor in Kenosha, Wisconsin, when James Langenbach used his car to try to kill two fourteen-year-old black youths. The victims, Austin Hansen-Tyler and Dontrell Langston, were riding bicycles and escaped serious injury. When Kenosha County circuit judge Michael Wilk sentenced Langenbach to 176 years in prison on April 25, 2002, he lectured him on what he had done: "It was a despicable act. There are no words that adequately describe the repugnance and revulsion that

The June 1998 attack and eventual murder of James Byrd Jr. was carried out for no other reason than because Byrd was an African American.

a civilized person should feel. You are deserving of the contempt and scorn of a civilized society."[22]

Racism "Is Always There"

Five centuries after the first black slaves were brought to the United States, acts of hatred and violence continue to plague African Americans. Native Americans, however, have suffered from racism even longer. In the 1500s, when Spanish, French, and English explorers arrived on the shores of the land that would become the United States, they were greeted by people who had already lived there for thousands of years. The languages, cultures, and physical characteristics of these Native Americans—they are

Hating the Chippewa

During the 1980s the Chippewa used treaty rights they had won a century earlier to use nets to catch walleyes in northern Wisconsin lakes. Whites were angry that they would not be able to catch as many fish in the same lakes and resorted to violent tactics to try to stop the Native Americans. Whites issued death threats to tribal leaders and staged protests in which they carried racist signs that read, "Save a Walleye, Spear a Pregnant Squaw." James Jannett, a tribal attorney for the Lac du Flambeau Chippewa, testified in 1988 about the violence against the Chippewa. His testimony is excerpted from Barbara Perry and Linda Robyn's article, "Putting Anti-Indian Violence in Context":

I was out by the boat landing one night where there was over a thousand people chanting racial things. One day we were setting the nets and they were throwing rocks and they were shooting, shooting wrist rockets, slingshots with ball bearings. One hit Sarah [Jannett's daughter] in her side, and knocked her to the bottom of the boat. I got hit too. We had people chase us, we had people follow us. We had threats, we had people pushing. [They] would throw lit cigarettes at us. They would spit on us, throw rocks.

Barbara Perry and Linda Robyn, "Putting Anti-Indian Violence in Context: The Case of the Great Lakes Chippewas of Wisconsin," *American Indian Quarterly*, Summer 2005, p. 628.

Racist policies against Native Americans have been in effect in the United States for centuries.

sometimes called First Americans or American Indians—all seemed strange to white Europeans. Europeans considered Native American cultures and religions inferior to European ways. Over the next three centuries, westward expansion of the United States to the Pacific Ocean came at the expense of Native Americans. White settlers and U.S. officials used their belief that they were superior to Indians to justify taking their homelands and confining them to reservations. Indians were not granted citizenship until 1924, when Congress passed the Indian Citizenship Act. The legislation was sparked by the heroic way in which thousands of Native Americans had fought for their country during World War I.

The new law, however, did not wipe out racism against American Indians. In the early hours of June 11, 2006, three white teenagers in Farmington, New Mexico, beat up forty-six-year-old William Blackie, a Navajo. Reports that the trio of attackers yelled racial slurs and made remarks that demeaned Blackie's Native American heritage did not surprise forty-seven-year-old Evan

Garfield, a Navajo friend of the victim. "It [racism] is always there,"[23] says Garfield.

NEGATIVE FEELINGS ABOUT NATIVE AMERICANS

"In 1999, 'Indian Hunting Season' flyers were distributed in South Dakota advertising an 'open season on the Sioux reservations' against 'worthless red bastards, dog eaters and prairie niggers.' The flyers set bag limits of 10 Indians per day with a limit of 40."

Valerie Taliman, "Hate Crime Shocks Paiute Reservation," *Indian Country Today,* March 2, 2005, p. A1.

Although the United States is the traditional homeland of Native Americans, the group's minority status and perceived physical and cultural differences set it apart from mainstream America. Such differences are usually most apparent among immigrant populations, such as Asians. Like Native Americans, Asians have suffered greatly throughout U.S. history. They faced hatred from the time they first began moving to the United States in large numbers during the mid-nineteenth century.

Prejudice Against Asians

Tens of thousands of Chinese began immigrating to the United States in 1848 after gold was discovered in California. For many decades, Chinese men and women were denied citizenship and other rights and were forced to live in segregated areas in cities. Some whites physically attacked Chinese men and women, and large groups sometimes invaded Chinatowns to burn and destroy businesses and homes.

Succeeding waves of immigrants from other Asian countries have faced similar racial hatred since then. Among the latest groups to face such animosity have been Southeast Asians from Vietnam, Laos, and Cambodia who fled to the United States after the Vietnam War ended in 1975 because they did not want to live under communism. On July 14, 2001, Thung Phetakoune, a sixty-two-year-old immigrant from Laos, was murdered in Newmarket, New Hampshire. Richard Labbe said he shot Phetakoune because "those Asians killed my brother and uncle in Vietnam. Call it payback."[24] Labbe was angry with the Asian Communists who had killed his relatives in combat. He targeted Phetakoune because his ethnicity and outward appearance matched Labbe's stereotypical image of an Asian Communist. Unfortunately, if Labbe had known anything about his victim—other than the fact that he was Southeast Asian—he would have realized that Phetakoune also hated Communists and had fled their rule in Laos.

Hatred of Asians was also a factor in a burglary in New Port Richey, Florida, on March 18, 2006. After police arrested Mark David Adge for breaking into an Asian market, they declared it was a hate crime because of the racial slurs Adge made while in custody.

"It Isn't Fair"

One of the most infamous cases of racial violence involved mistaken identity. In 1982 two white men in Detroit beat to death a Chinese man named Vincent Chin because they thought he was Japanese. They hated Asians because sales of Japanese automobiles had forced U.S. companies to lay off workers. In her online article for USAsians.net, Christine Ho recounts how Chin died:

> "It Isn't Fair." These words were Vincent Chin's last before he lost consciousness. On June 19, 1982, Chin, a 27-year-old Chinese American, was beaten to death with a baseball bat in Detroit [by] Ronald Ebens and Michael Nitz, who blamed Japanese carmakers for Detroit's problems in

the auto industry. Ebens was heard saying, "It is because of you little [expletives] that we're out of work!" [Ebens] hit Chin several times with the bat on the back and head causing Chin to fall on the ground. Fighting continued with Ebens as the aggressor. [Chin] lapsed into a severe coma, and after emergency surgery, he was pronounced brain dead. Four days later on June 23, 1982, the ventilator through which he was breathing was removed and he died.

Christine Ho, "The Model Minority Awakened: The Murder of Vincent Chin." http://us_asians.tripod.com/articles-vincentchin.html.

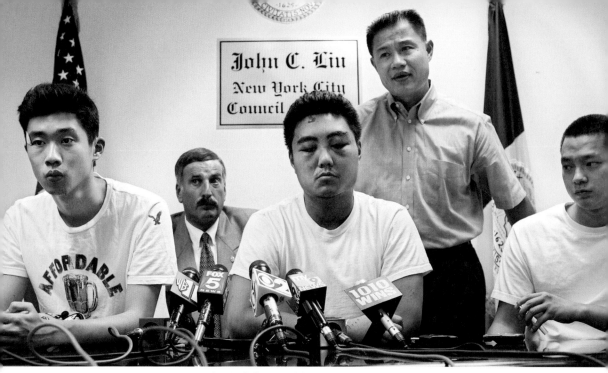

Asian Americans John Lu, left, Reynold Liang, center, and David Wu were assaulted in August 2006. The men believe they were the victims of a hate crime based on their ethnicity.

Adge's hatred of Asians was the motivation for the crime. Like the majority of people who commit hate crimes, Adge is white. But blacks, Asians, and members of other racial groups who are often victims of hate crimes also have prejudices, and they too commit hate crimes.

Not Only Whites Are Racists

On June 5, 2006, while Kim McCandless was trying to find a parking spot in the Sunrise Mall in Massapequa, New York, Carl Graves threw a chunk of cement at her vehicle. The twenty-year-old black man acted because he was angry that whites were shopping at his neighborhood mall. McCandless was upset that the four small children with her could have been hurt. She was even angrier when she learned why she was attacked: "To know it's about a skin color bothers me even more."[25] Graves was charged with a hate crime.

Some blacks attack whites to seek vengeance for white racism. On October 7, 1989, in Kenosha, Wisconsin, a group of black men watched *Mississippi Burning*, a film about white racists killing a black civil rights worker. Afterward, when they saw a fourteen-year-old white boy walking down the street, nineteen-year-old Todd Mitchell asked the other men, "Do you all feel hyped up to move on some white people?"[26] The blacks decided to take out their anger over what they had seen in the movie on the youth. They beat him severely and stole his tennis shoes.

Blacks and Hispanics sometimes commit hate crimes against each other. In Los Angeles, California, four members of a Latino gang were charged with a hate crime for murdering Kenneth Wilson. On June 27, 2006, assistant U.S. attorney Alex Busta-mante said during their trial that they killed Wilson "because he was black [and] gang members had promised each other, had agreed that they would drive African Americans out of the neighborhood, by threats, by force, by murder."[27] Bustamante said the murder was part of a six-year gang effort to keep blacks from moving to their neighborhood. All four defendants were convicted. The reason they were charged with hate crimes in addition to first-degree murder is because the consequences of such acts of hatred are not confined to an individual victim.

The Harm Racist Hate Crimes Cause

Columbia University law professor Kent Greenawalt states that hate crimes not only harm the victim but also other people of the same race by frightening, humiliating, or intimidating them. Wilson's murder was a warning to all blacks that they were not welcome and would not be safe in the neighborhood the Latino gang claimed as its own. Cross burnings are an example of a hate crime that affects an entire racial group. In an opinion defending a Virginia law that outlaws cross burnings, U.S. Supreme Court justice Clarence Thomas, an African American, declared, "There is no other purpose to the [burning] cross—no communication, no particular message. It was intended to cause fear and to terrorize a population."[28] Such acts also divide communities by increasing tensions among all white and black residents.

The greatest harm that hate crimes cause, however, is to victims and their families. In July 2004 Asian-hating whites in San Francisco attacked Jeff Woo and four of his friends because they were Chinese. The assault made Asians fearful of the area in which the attack occurred. It also saddened them because the incident showed how much some people hated them. "We'll never forget," Woo said. "It's still inside us."[29]

A similar incident of racial hatred occurred during the 1999 Fourth of July holiday weekend in Illinois. Ricky Byrdsong was one of two victims shot to death during a shooting spree by Benjamin Nathaniel Smith, a racist who hated blacks. Byrdsong's widow, Sherialyn, remembers how hard it was to tell her three children that their father was dead and to disclose the manner in which he was killed. Byrdsong says, "I will never forget the look on their faces and their screams of horror and disbelief."[30]

A HATE CRIME PERPETRATOR CONFESSES

"I said to myself, 'The first person that I see in this mall that looks white, I'm killing.' I had never seen this woman before and I didn't care. All I knew was she had blond hair and blue eyes and she had to die."

The confession of Phillip Grant, a black man found guilty on July 11, 2006, of killing Concetta Russo-Carriero. Quoted in Anahad O'Connor, "Homeless Man Is Convicted of Murder as a Hate Crime," *New York Times*, July 12, 2006, p. B5.

Even the people who commit such crimes suffer when they are punished. On June 23, 2006, Abel Castaneda was sentenced to ten years in prison for beating up Steve Lawson. Castaneda attacked Lawson in Santa Ana, California, for one reason: Lawson is black. When Castaneda was sentenced, he told Lawson, "I'm sorry for what happened. Now we are both paying the price."[31]

"No One Deserves This"

Although hate-crime perpetrators like Castaneda have earned their punishment by breaking the law, their targets are innocent victims who have done nothing to merit such abuse. After James Langenbach was sentenced to 176 years in prison on April 25, 2002, for trying to run down Austin Hansen-Tyler and Dontrell Langston, Roechita Tyler said she could not understand why Langenbach had tried to harm her son just because he was black. "Because no one deserves this. No one deserves this,"[32] she said.

HATE CRIMES BASED ON RELIGION

Forty Muslim men were kneeling reverently in prayer at the Lewiston-Auburn Islamic Center in Maine on July 3, 2006, when Brent Matthews rolled a severed pig's head into their midst. Matthews claimed it was a prank, but his act was a religious hate crime. Muslims believe pigs are unclean and consider physical contact with them offensive; the pig head not only interrupted the Muslims' prayers but also defiled their place of worship. Ibrahim Hooper, spokesman for the national Council on American-Islamic Relations, says the act violated the right of religious freedom guaranteed by the U.S. Constitution. Hooper contends, "All Americans should be able to offer prayers in their houses of worship without fear of attack or intimidation."[33]

"MUTUAL RESPECT AND TOLERANCE" ARE MANDATORY

"I want to understand this to find out why we are seeing more intolerance in our society, in this particular case directed at a particular community. We can't get along in this country unless we have mutual respect and tolerance for each other."

Senator Bill Nelson commenting on an increase in hate crimes against Jews. Quoted in George Bennett, "Nelson Pushing Broader Federal Hate Crime Law," *Palm Beach (FL) Post,* April 12, 2006, p. B3.

The hate crime was only one of many that have been directed against Muslims since the September 11, 2001, attacks on the United States by the Muslim terrorist group al Qaeda. But Muslims are not the only people who are attacked for their religious beliefs.

Religious beliefs often divide people and cause some of them to hate those who follow other religions.

Each year there are hundreds of such criminal offenses against Jews, Christians, and members of other faiths.

The Source of Religious Hatred

One of the most important themes in Christianity, Judaism, and Islam, as well as other religions, is that people should love and respect each other. But psychologist Ervin Staub argues that despite that central message, religious beliefs often divide people and cause some of them to hate those who follow other religions. According to Staub, "Religions, which proclaim love but at the same time almost always identify other religions as false and as the wrong way to worship God, have been both a frequent basis of differentiating *us* and *them* and a source of hate for those of other faiths."[34] For thousands of years, members of the world's three major religions—Christianity, Judaism, and Islam—have at times hated and warred against each other because they believe their conception of God is the only true one. Individual religions have also been divided over the proper way to worship the same God. Roman Catholicism and Protestantism are both Christian religions, but their members have often clashed because of differences in some of their beliefs and traditional ways of worship.

Followers of Jewish, Christian, and Muslim religions brought those ancient hatreds with them when they immigrated to the United States, a fact that is reflected in statistics on U.S. religious hate crimes. In *Hate Crime Statistics 2005*, the Federal Bureau of Investigation reported 1,227 hate-crime incidents involving 1,314 criminal offenses that were motivated by religious bias. The victims included 977 Jews, 151 Muslims, 61 Catholics, and 58 Protestants. A total of 106 hate-crime victims were of other religions, such as Hinduism and Buddhism. Most of those twenty-first-century crimes were similar to hateful acts that members of various religions have committed against each other for centuries. The religious bias that is responsible for more such acts than any other is anti-Semitism, the name for hatred of Jews.

Hate Crimes Against Jews

On March 4, 2006, unknown vandals painted eleven large swastikas on the Striar Jewish Community Center in Stoughton, Massachusetts. The swastika, the best-known symbol of Nazi Germany, is a bitter reminder to Jews of the Holocaust, when the Nazis murdered 11 million people, including 6 million Jews, during

Defacing homes, synagogues, and other buildings with swastikas is one of the most common hate crimes against Jews.

World War II (1939–45). Defacing homes, synagogues, and other buildings with swastikas is one of the most common hate crimes against Jews Such acts continue a centuries-old pattern of anti-Semitism in the United States.

UN-AMERICAN BEHAVIOR IN AMERICA

"We live in a pluralistic society where the free exercise of religion is one of the central tenets of our society. When a population within that American fabric feels targeted based solely on their religious beliefs, we believe that to be not only illegal but also un-American."

Arsalan Iftikhar, legal director for the Council on American-Islamic Relations, explains that religious freedom is one of the key freedoms the United States guarantees its citizens. Quoted in David Hency, "Prosecutors Have Options in Mosque Case," *Portland (ME) Press Herald*, July 12, 2006, p. B1.

Large numbers of Jewish people did not begin immigrating to the United States until the late nineteenth century. Although even the few who arrived earlier had met with some hostility, anti-Semitism increased and grew stronger as the number of Jewish immigrants grew. This hatred resulted in job and social discrimination against Jews, who also became targets of violence that today would be considered hate crimes. Anti-Semites, including members of the Ku Klux Klan (KKK)—which hated Jews as well as blacks—beat up or murdered Jewish people and burned down synagogues. Today KKK groups continue to target Jews for hate crimes, as do neo-Nazi groups that promote German leader Adolf Hitler's racial and religious ideas that led to the Holocaust.

Christians have committed most of the hate crimes against Jews. The traditional basis for Christian anti-Semitism is the belief that Jews were responsible for killing Jesus Christ, even though it was a Roman official who ordered his death and Roman soldiers who crucified him. In 2004 actor Mel Gibson was accused of anti-Semitism for promoting this claim in his controversial film *The Passion of the Christ*. Gibson denied then that he hated Jews, but an incident two years later raised new questions about his beliefs. On July 28, 2006, Los Angeles County sheriff's deputy James Mee arrested Gibson for speeding and drunk driving. In his official report, Mee writes that Gibson threatened him, "blurted out a barrage of anti-Semitic remarks about [profanity deleted] Jews," and claimed "the Jews are responsible for all the wars in the world." Gibson then asked Mee, "Are you a Jew?"[35] Mee is Jewish. Gibson was so hostile that Mee requested help from other officers to arrest him.

During the late twentieth century, increased immigration by Muslims brought more people to the United States who hated Jews. Judaism and Islam both began in the Middle East, and for centuries the two religions have been bitter rivals over which religion is the true one. This hatred gained strength in the early twenty-first century as the Jewish nation of Israel and the Muslim countries that surround it continued to clash. Anger over that situation led a few Muslims living in the United States to vandalize synagogues and attack Jews.

An example of this occurred on July 28, 2006, when Naveed Afzal Haq killed one woman and wounded five others in a shooting rampage at the Jewish Federation of Greater Seattle in Washington. After Haq had taken people at the center hostage, he called an emergency 911 dispatcher. Haq said he hated Jews because Muslims were dying in Israel's battles with its neighbors and in the Iraq War. Although the war was waged by the United States and its allies, Haq blamed Jews for the fighting. He told the

Incidents of Jewish/Islamic violence in the United States, such as the 2006 shooting at the Jewish Federation of Greater Seattle by a Muslim man, have increased especially since the start of the Iraq War.

operator, "These are Jews, and I'm tired of . . . our people getting pushed around by the situation in the Middle East."[36]

Terrorism and Islamophobia

The war in Iraq, which helped incite Haq's shooting spree, was also the main reason for many hate crimes against American Muslims. When al Qaeda attacked the United States on September 11, 2001, the country's estimated 6 million American Muslims became targets for people angry at the Muslim terrorist group. In the first month after the attacks, more than three hundred hate crimes against Muslims occurred in thirty-eight states. By the end of 2001 the number of such offenses had nearly tripled. People shouted slurs at Muslims; made telephoned death threats; vandalized and set fire to Muslim mosques, homes, and businesses; and beat up

A Cause for Hating Muslims

According to sociologists Jack Levin and Jack McDevitt, "On September 11, 2001, Americans witnessed the most violent single incident of hate-motivated violence in this country's history." They were referring to the attack by the Muslim terrorist group al Qaeda. They also claim that the attack showed how one incident could create a climate that would foster thousands of hate crimes:

> If we were ever unsure, the September 11 [2001] attack on America provided indisputable evidence that a single situation can precipitate major changes in the ways that we behave toward the groups in our midst. In the aftermath of the dev-

astation created by Middle Eastern terrorists, Americans of Arab descent or Islamic religious beliefs who had previously lived in relative peace and tranquillity abruptly found themselves at great personal risk. Prejudiced feelings and beliefs about Arabs and Muslims, long hidden from view, suddenly were expressed in a generalized suspicion of anyone of Middle Eastern heritage. This suspicion was played out in violent acts across the country ranging from simple assault to murder.

Jack Levin and Jack McDevitt, *Hate Crimes Revisited: America's War Against Those Who Are Different.* Cambridge, MA: Westview, 2002, p. 3.

Reported Incidents Against Arabs and Muslims in the United States, by Category September 11, 2001–February 8, 2002

Type of Incident	Number
Airport Profiling	191
Bomb Threats	16
Deaths	11
Death Threats	56
Discrimination at Schools	74
Discrimination at Work	166
Hate Mail	315
Intimidation by Law Enforcement	224
Physical Assault/Property Damage	289
Public Harassment	372
Total Incidents	1,714

In the months after the September 11, 2001, terrorist attacks against the United States, the number of hate crimes against Muslim Americans significantly increased.

Muslims. In several incidents, American Muslims were even murdered. These incidents happened despite the fact that American Muslims had condemned the attack, which had killed Muslims as well as members of other religions.

Although the pace of hate crimes against Muslims slowed after 2001, Muslims continued to be targeted for the next several years. Anti-Muslim feeling remained high in the United States because of the nation's continuing war against al Qaeda and other Muslim terrorist groups, which included invasions of Afghanistan and Iraq. Combat deaths of U.S. soldiers in those two countries were a major source of Muslim hatred, even though many American Muslims also fought and died for their country during the war.

In the first few years of the twenty-first century, hatred against
Muslims in the United States and other countries grew so strong
that a term was coined to describe it—*Islamophobia*. On December
7, 2004, the United Nations (UN) met to discuss how to ease such
fear and hatred. Muslim journalist Mouin Rabbani attended the
UN seminar and admitted that the September 11 attack had greatly strengthened anti-Muslim feelings that had already existed. He
said at the time, "My impression is that hostility to Islam as a religion has grown exponentially. A main effect of 9-11 has been to
make [hatred of Muslims] not only more widespread but also con-
siderably more mainstream and respectable—it has let the genie
out of the bottle."[37]

Attacks Against Muslims

Many of the crimes this hatred has generated have been directed
against the Muslim religion. Thousands of mosques in the United
States became the main targets of people who hated Muslims.
During the first few years after September 11, 2001, scores of these
places of worship were vandalized with graffiti or damaged by

*Islamophobia is a term that was coined in the wake of September 11, 2001, to
describe the growing anti-Muslim sentiment in the United States and other
countries.*

In the United States, attacks on mosques and desecration of the Koran, the Muslim holy book, are the most prevalent hate crimes committed against Muslims.

arson fires and bombs; in Florida, one man smashed his truck into the Islamic Center of Tallahassee. In April 2006 shots were fired into a Maryland mosque, and in June 2006 a sign that claimed "Muslims Worship Satan" was left near an Arizona mosque.

Another way to attack Islam is to desecrate the Koran, the Muslim holy book. People have burned the Koran or have spit on it in public displays of hate. In July 2006 a copy of the Koran that had been riddled with bullets was tossed onto the steps of the Islamic Center of Chattanooga, Tennessee. The perpetrator also posted a video on the Internet that showed the book being struck by bullets. On July 10, 2006, Arsalan Iftikhar, the legal director of the Council on American-Islamic Relations, condemned the incident. He claimed it was not only a hate crime but also a violation of the Muslims' right to freedom of religion. According to Iftikhar, "By throwing the bullet-riddled Quran [Koran] at the mosque, we believe the perpetrators went beyond the limits of free speech by taking part in an overt act of religious intimidation."[38]

Hating Catholics

The United States is a predominantly Christian nation, and Christians have committed most of the hate crimes against Jews and Muslims. But one Christian group has been targeted by other Christians—Roman Catholics. Catholics have faced religious discrimination and hate crimes since the 1600s, when they first began immigrating to the English colonies that would one day become the United States. Most hatred has come from Protestants, members of a separate branch of Christianity who disagree with some Catholic beliefs and forms of worship. Protestants dominated the colonies, and at times they barred Catholics from practicing their faith. When large numbers of Irish and European Catholics began immigrating to the United States during the nineteenth century, Protestants used their economic and political power to discriminate against Catholics in jobs and housing. Protestant gangs also attacked Catholics and their churches, sometimes destroying the churches.

HATE CRIME COMMITTED AGAINST A CHURCH

"I think it's despicable, sad, and terrible. It's such a bad thing. It really troubles me. We need to get to the bottom of it. It seems a very heinous crime."

Rocco J. Longo, town manager in Duxbury, Massachusetts, about a wooden cross that was set on fire at Holy Family Catholic Church. Quoted in David Abel, "Burning of Cross Probed as Hate Crime," *Boston Globe,* February 22, 2005, p. B2.

This hatred eased in the twentieth century, and in 1960 John F. Kennedy overcame this prejudice to become the first Catholic president. But anti-Catholic incidents sometimes still occur, like the one that happened on June 6, 2006, at Holy Hill, a Catholic shrine near Milwaukee, Wisconsin. Two men, who were later arrested, spray-painted "Hell Will Rule" and "I'm Glad They Killed Jesus" on religious statues. During a mass several days later at Holy Hill, Milwaukee archbishop Timothy Dolan told more than 750 people that the "gross acts of desecration" were a reminder that hatred and evil still exist. "We trust that the invincible power of Christ will reclaim this sanctuary from the forces of evil,"[39] Dolan said.

A new source of Catholic hatred arose in the 1990s when scores of priests were charged with sexually assaulting young boys, usually in incidents that had occurred decades ago. In the years since then, some hate crimes aimed at the Catholic Church have been linked to outrage over this sexual misconduct. In November 2002 someone in Everett, Massachusetts, scrawled *whore* on a statue of Mary, the mother of Jesus Christ, and spray-painted a profanity and the word *lies* on the front doors of Our Lady of Grace Catholic Church. A former pastor of the church had been accused of sexually molesting children. Donna Morrissey, a church spokeswoman, says even though the former pastor's actions might have made people angry, "I would condemn any kind of desecration of a house of worship or a statue or an incident such as this."[40]

Religious Hate Crimes Affect All Religions

Although most religious hate crimes involve the three major religions—Christianity, Judaism, and Islam—attacks on smaller religious groups also occur. On April 5, 2006, vandals struck a Hindu temple that was under construction in the Minneapolis suburb of Maple Grove, Minnesota. The attack resulted in damages totaling two hundred thousand dollars and included the destruction of

Defiling a place of worship, a place that believers consider sacred, is an especially heinous act of hatred.

Hating the Amish

The Amish are Christians who are targeted for hate crimes because their religion makes them shun modern conveniences like telephones, electricity, and automobiles. The Amish live in many rural areas in the United States. Their simple life makes them seem strange to other people, who sometimes shoot at their horse-drawn buggies. In January 2006 two teenagers in Taylor County, Wisconsin, shot paintball guns at Amish homes, damaged mailboxes, and heaved a cement block through the window of an Amish furniture store. They were charged with criminal damage to property and disorderly conduct as hate crimes. When nineteen-year-old Cody J. Bunkelman was arrested, he apologized but was quoted as saying "A lot of people mess around with the Amish." Taylor County district attorney Karl Kelz responded to the crimes by saying they were something that could not be tolerated. He is quoted in Luke Klink's article for the *Milwaukee Journal Sentinel* as saying, "I am bothered by a kid who said, 'Let's go pick on the Amish.' You might as well strike out the word Amish and insert blacks, Jews, Muslims or Catholics. Rural Wisconsin can't afford to have us say, 'Don't worry about it.' That is not a good message to send."

Luke Klink, "Teens Accused of Targeting Amish," *Milwaukee Journal Sentinel,* January 5, 2006, p. 3B.

important statues depicting religious deities. The vandalism forced postponement of the opening of the temple for several months, affecting the more than twenty thousand Hindus in Minnesota, North Dakota, South Dakota, and Iowa who wanted to pray in the new temple. "It is an enormous tragedy. Nobody expects such things in a tolerant state like Minnesota,"[41] said Minnesota state senator Satveer Chaudhury, a Hindu.

Such hate crimes do more harm than merely damaging places of worship. They also create mental and emotional anguish for the members of that religion. After vandals threw bricks through four windows at the Metropolitan Baptist Church in Altadena, California, in March 2006, Earl Perry, the chairman of the church's board of trustees, was upset that any person would defile a place of worship. Perry says, "It's disturbing that anyone would attack a church, to me. I was brought up to believe that the ground where a church is, is sacred, and it's hands off. I guess I'm a little old-fashioned in that."[42]

HATE CRIMES BASED ON SEXUAL ORIENTATION

During a party in Edgewood, New Mexico, on June 29, 2006, several people began making fun of a gay man. When he tried to leave the party, three men forced him and a female friend to walk to a nearby deserted field. There, the trio pushed the man up against a fence and began hitting and kicking him. In a beating that lasted several hours, the man suffered bleeding on the brain, a concussion, facial lacerations, and bruising. When William York, age twenty-one, was arrested on multiple charges in the attack, he told authorities he wanted to "scare" his gay victim so badly that the experience would "make him straight and get him to stop acting the way he was."[43]

The New Mexico homosexual was one of thousands of men and women in the United States who are victims of hate crimes each year because of their sexual orientation. The majority of offenses are against homosexuals and lesbians, people who choose members of their own gender as sexual partners. Hate crimes are also committed against bisexuals, heterosexuals, transgender people, and transsexuals. Transgender people are men and women who are born one sex but believe the opposite gender is the correct one for them; they often dress and live as members of that gender. Transsexuals are men or women who also believe the opposite gender is the correct one for them but have had surgery to acquire the physical characteristics of that gender. The term *transgender* is often used to refer to both transsexuals and transgenders.

Mark Potok is editor of the *Intelligence Report,* which is published by the Southern Poverty Law Center. The magazine monitors the activities of groups that commit hate crimes against all types of people. Potok believes that transsexuals and transgenders suffer more than any other group that is hated because of its differences: "None are so victimized as the transgender community. These men and women—from cross-dressers to those who have undergone sex change operations—may be the most despised people in America."[44]

How Many Hate Crimes?

The bitter hatred of transgenders results in some of the most brutal murders associated with any category of hate crimes. Yet these sensational homicides are only a small percentage of the total number of offenses caused by hatred of a person's sexual preference or gender identity. In *Hate Crime Statistics 2005*, the Federal Bureau of Investigation lists 1,197 sexual-orientation hate crimes. These incidents involved 1,171 criminal offenses, 1,213 victims, and 1,138 known offenders. The vast majority of offenses were against male homosexuals (713) and lesbians (183), and 228 crimes involved a bias against male or female homosexuality in general instead of against a specific individual. In addition, 23 offenses occurred against heterosexuals and 27 against bisexuals. The annual report

Hatred of people for their sexual orientation is widespread. And members of what is known as the lesbian, gay, bisexual, and transgender (LGBT) community must deal with this hate every day of their lives.

The Scope of Sexual-Orientation Violence

Members of the lesbian, gay, bisexual, and transgender (LGBT) community live daily with the threat of violence from people who hate them. The National Coalition of Anti-Violence Programs (NCAVP) explains that sexual-orientation violence takes many forms, from bullying in school to rape, sexual assault, and murder. The NCAVP states that there is so much hatred based on sexual orientation that almost every LGBT individual will become a victim of a hate crime or hate incident:

> The best available research suggests that 40 percent of lesbians and gay men in the U.S. consider themselves the victims of hate violence in their adult lifetimes, and that hate violence is a near-universal experience of openly LGBT youth. [Even] the minority of LGBT people who do not personally experience [hate crimes] or other characteristic forms of violence (which include sexual assaults and abuse, "pick-up" crimes, family abuse and police misconduct) may suffer the secondary effects, when friends or family members are targeted or when they limit their own freedom or self-expression because they fear becoming victims themselves.

National Coalition of Anti-Violence Programs, "What Does NCAVP Do?" www.ncavp.org/about/default.aspx.

does not separately list incidents involving transgender people; it includes such offenses under the categories of either homosexual or lesbian, depending on the victim's gender.

Gregory M. Herek, a psychology professor at the University of California, Davis, is an expert on sexual-orientation hate crimes. He believes federal statistics paint a flawed portrait of the frequency of such offenses because many victims never report them to officials. Herek says, "Estimates of nonreporting among gay and lesbian hate crime victims [in various studies] have ranged as high as 90 percent."[45] Herek says that many victims do not report crimes because they believe law enforcement officials will discriminate against or mistreat them, a fear that is based on past incidents in which this has sometimes happened. Many victims also fear that they will suffer negative consequences from employers, friends, or even spouses if their sexual orientation is publicly revealed in a criminal complaint.

Another reason why such hate crimes are underreported is because law enforcement officials and the justice system often do not categorize them as such offenses. The brutal October 2002 slaying in Newark, California, of Gwen Araujo is an example of this. Edward Araujo Jr., a seventeen-year-old boy who lived as a woman, was kicked and beaten with an iron skillet, struck with a shovel, and choked with a rope. On September 12, 2005, a jury convicted two men of second-degree murder in Araujo's death but found them innocent of hate-crime charges. Thom Lynch, executive director of the San Francisco Lesbian, Gay, Bisexual, and Transgender Community Center, criticizes that verdict: "Only some justice has been done. The idea that hate was not a factor [in Araujo's death] is just unimaginable."[46] But because the two men had had sex with Araujo, the jury decided the murder was motivated by their anger over discovering that Araujo was a man and not by a hatred of transgenders.

No One Deserves to Be a Victim

"Whether you're a prostitute, a bus driver, a retired U.S. Capitol police officer—all of whom I know as transgendered people— you don't deserve to be the victim of a crime."

Metropolitan police sergeant Brett Parson, interview, "On the Streets," *Intelligence Report,* Winter 2003. www.splcenter.org/intel/intelreport/article.jsp?aid=150.

Despite whether such offenses are officially considered hate crimes, hatred of people for their sexual orientation is widespread. And members of what is known as the lesbian, gay, bisexual, and transgender (LGBT) community must deal with this hate every day of their lives.

Hate Crimes in Schools

School is the first place in which many people are exposed to hatred because they are different. This is especially true for LGBT people, who are often cruelly mocked or physically abused because of their sexual or gender orientation. Debra Chasnoff works in schools to promote understanding of LGBT students. She writes that LGBT students are often the targets of hate crimes:

[LGBT] students hear anti-gay slurs such as "homo," "faggot," and "sissy" about 26 times a day, or once every 14 minutes. More than 30 percent of LGBT youth are threatened or injured at school in any given year. And for every LGBT student who reports being harassed, four straight students said they were harassed just because they were perceived to be gay or lesbian.[47]

THE MESSAGE BEHIND HATE CRIMES

"Hate crimes are message crimes, and the message is: You and your kind don't belong here. They are intended to create fear and isolation."

Dane County district attorney Brian Blanchard commenting on hate crimes against gays in Madison, Wisconsin. Quoted in Anita Clark, "Marriage Bill Debate Stirs Fears," *Wisconsin State Journal,* April 24, 2006, p. B1.

LGBT students are also targets of hate when they attend colleges and universities. Many of the hateful acts directed against them occur in dormitories that they share with heterosexual students. One such incident occurred in Madison, Wisconsin. While yelling, "All faggots should die," four students ripped down posters that were taped to a gay University of Wisconsin student's door. The men also spit on the door and wrote on it, "I hate [expletive] faggots. Die."[48] In January 2006 the four students were charged with disorderly conduct and criminal damage to property as hate crimes.

Attacking Gays Anywhere

Unfortunately, LGBT students do not leave behind such hatred when they graduate. It follows them the rest of their lives. Heyward Drummond knows this all too well. When Drummond, who lives in Aldie, Virginia, went to get his newspaper on the morning of July 29, 2006, he saw that vandals had written the word *fag* on his driveway, mailbox, and a nearby fence. They had also poured gasoline on his lawn and destroyed flowers and trees. "I just don't understand how someone could hate like that,"[49] Drummond says. But Drummond did understand that the reason for the destruction was that someone hated the fact that he and his domestic partner, John Ellis, lived in the upscale neighborhood.

Being attacked at home makes people feel especially vulnerable because home is where most people expect to feel safest. But a 2002 study on sexual-orientation hate crimes published in the *Journal of Social Issues* showed that LGBT people fear being attacked anywhere and at any time. One example the study cited was a woman and some friends who went to a public park one day and were beaten by three men because they were lesbians. The woman explains what happened:

> When [a friend] said she didn't want to fight, he just stuck his fist out and broke her nose. As he was getting ready to throw the punch he said "[expletive] dykes." One person [got] a cut open on their face. And another one had her collarbone broken and got knocked unconscious. I got kicked in the knee and upper thigh and was

Watching a Gay Friend Die

In a 2002 study of hate crimes based on sexual orientation, one gay man explained how he was beaten and his friend was killed when they were attacked by six men outside a bar in an unnamed southern town. The two victims were walking to their car in the bar's parking lot with two friends when six men began calling them "fags" and then started beating them. The survivor explains what happened:

> My friend was hit in the head with a brick, and when he went down, they hit him more in the head with bricks and clubs till he stopped moving. I

was hit in the legs with a club, and broke my knee cap. The other two friends got away and went back into the bar to call the police, and came out with more people from the bar, and chased the attackers away until the police got there. The police took about 20 minutes to get there and the ambulance almost a half an hour. By that time [my friend] had already expired. He died in my arms.

Quoted in Gregory M. Herek, Jeanine C. Cogan, and J. Roy Gillis, "Victim Experiences in Hate Crimes Based on Sexual Orientation," *Journal of Social Issues*, 2002, vol. 58, p. 329.

Gay bashing is when perpetrators actively seek out gay and lesbian victims to hurt. Such was the case in 2006 at Puzzles Lounge in New Bedford, Massachusetts.

severely bruised. And then somebody came by and helped scare them away.[50]

Although many hate crimes are the result of such chance encounters, predators sometimes seek out LGBT individuals in what is known as *gay bashing*. This happened on February 2, 2006, when Jacob Robida, age eighteen, went to Puzzles Lounge, a gay bar in New Bedford, Massachusetts. In a savage attack, Robida wounded two men with a hatchet and shot a third man before fleeing the establishment; the three men later recovered from their injuries. A bartender described the attack: "He started swinging the hatchet on top of this customer's head. He just had a stone-cold look on his face . . . just emotionless."[51] Two days later Robida killed himself and a companion after police stopped their car in Arkansas. The shoot-out ended a manhunt for Robida that had swept through several states.

"Disposable People"

Although many groups incur hate-crime vandalism and violence, it is believed that hate-related murder rates are highest for victims belonging to the LGBT community. And none are attacked as often or as savagely as transgenders. In a story about violence against transgender individuals, the *Intelligence Report* noted that in 2002 the FBI reported eleven hate-crime murders motivated by racial, religious, or sexual-orientation bias. In contrast, the magazine said a study it conducted based on news accounts, police reports, and other sources had documented at least fourteen murders of transgender people in that same year. The discrepancy was due to federal officials attributing some of the murders to motives other than hatred over sexual orientation.

Transgender violence is especially high in Washington, D.C. In August 2003 two transgender women were shot and killed and several others were attacked. Jessica Xavier, a transgender activist in the nation's capital, claimed then that transgender violence had reached an all-time high in Washington, D.C.: "What we're seeing is a war against transgendered women. We are regarded by most as disposable people."[52] To support her claim, Xavier cited results of a study she conducted in 2000. Of four thousand transgender people who were interviewed, 17 percent said they had been assaulted with a weapon because of their gender identity.

A TEENAGER SPEAKS OUT

"I guess I always kind of knew that I was a lesbian. At school, people would make fun of me [and] it got to me after a while. I feel very self-conscious about that."

A Santa Fe, New Mexico, teenager talking about being bullied. Quoted in Teresa Baca, "Monologues Give Insight to Teens Who Are 'Out,'" *Santa Fe New Mexican,* June 9, 2006, p. D3.

Most transgender hate crimes involve men who are posing as or have surgically become women. However, one of the most famous transgender hate crimes involves a woman who lived as a man. On December 31, 1993, Brandon Teena and two friends—Lisa Lambert and Philip De Vine—were shot and stabbed to death in rural Falls City, Nebraska. Brandon Teena was born a woman named Teena Renae Brandon, but she chose to live as a man. Teena was dating Lambert and several other women when John Lotter and Marvin Thomas Nissen discovered her true gender. They were so angry that a woman was posing as a man that they raped her. After Teena reported the rape to police, the men killed her and her two friends.

The brutal incident received widespread media coverage. Gwen Smith, whose Internet site, Remembering Our Dead, tracks transgender violence, says the death helped raise awareness of such hate crimes and spurred action to stop them. Smith recalls, "It was very shocking and it was a wake-up call. After it happened the transgender community began to get together and start working on things."[53] The 1999 movie *Boys Don't Cry,* starring Hilary Swank as Brandon Teena, also helped publicize transgender violence.

Living in Fear

Violent attacks like the one that led to Teena's death are more common against members of the LGBT community than they are against any other group targeted by hate crimes. The extreme brutality that often accompanies these assaults makes many LGBT people live in constant fear. Sara Henriksen was harassed while attending Waterloo High School in Iowa because she was a lesbian. After she was beaten up, Henriksen constantly worried about being attacked again. During a March 1, 2006, conference on gay hate crimes in Iowa, the Waterloo senior admitted that she was afraid while attending school: "I wonder if the footsteps in the hall are those of the [next] person who'll hurt me."[54] Her concern was heightened by hateful notes that fellow students stuffed in her locker.

The possibility that they will be murdered—the ultimate act of violence—is something LGBT people know is a possibility. In June 2006 a pickup truck bearing the sign "I believe all homosexals [sic] should be hunted down and killed" was seen driving through the streets of Fort Collins, Colorado. Most people never

Teena Brandon, a transgendered woman, chose to live her life as a man. She was killed in 1993 by two men who were angry upon learning her true gender.

have to worry about such threats, but some men and women in Fort Collins were afraid they would be singled out because of their sexual orientation. Diana Wess, a gay-rights spokeswoman, wrote to the *Coloradoan* newspaper to condemn the hateful act. In her letter, Wess asked readers to "imagine yourself as the target of this threatening message."[55]

A Judge's Moral Verdict

Wess's letter helped people understand how hateful messages hurt and upset gay people. In a similar manner, a Michigan judge tried to make a man convicted of murdering a homosexual realize how terrible his crime had been. On August 8, 2006, Wayne County circuit judge David Allen sentenced seventeen-year-old Steven

Caitlin Muese, a fifteen-year-old high school sophomore, was the victim of an alleged gay-bashing attack. The extreme brutality that often accompanies these attacks makes many in the gay community live in constant fear.

Williams Jr. of Detroit, Michigan, to twelve years in prison for shooting thirty-one-year-old Salvagio Vonatti of Windsor, Ontario, who is gay. In December 2005 Williams had shot Vonatti in the head outside of a Detroit gay bar. When Allen sentenced Williams for assault with intent to do great bodily harm and for using a firearm to commit a felony, Vonatti was still in a coma and was not expected to recover. Calling the attack a gay hate crime, Allen told Williams that the things he and the victim had in common were greater than their differences:

> Like you [Vonatti] is a son, brother, uncle, cousin, friend and lover. He loved and was loved and was on this earth to be left alone in peace and happiness. Who and how he loved was none of your business and was no threat to you and the community. Let's also get one other thing straight that came up in trial. Homosexuality is not a "lifestyle" or "choice." Homosexuality is no different than the color of your eyes or hair. [Would] anyone in their right mind choose to be homosexual with predators like you shooting them in the head for being gay? [56]

CHAPTER 5

HATING IMMIGRANTS, THE DISABLED, AND THE HOMELESS

O n April 28, 2006, a fifteen-year-old Latino student was walking to school in Salt Lake City, Utah, when two white men pulled up in a car and attacked him. Yelling racist comments, including "stupid Mexican" and "We don't want no Mexicans here,"[57] the men beat him and then drove away. The student suffered cuts, bruises, and three fractures to his left eye socket. Eight days later, at a Ku Klux Klan rally in Russelville, Alabama, Klansmen burned a 22-foot-high (6.7m) cross while shouting, "Let's get rid of the Mexicans!"[58]

These incidents were part of a wave of hate speech and hate crimes against Mexicans and other Latinos that swept the United States in the first few years of the twenty-first century. Latinos, however, were just one group that was targeted because of xenophobia, the fear and hatred of people who were born in other countries or share a distinct ethnic heritage.

Ethnic and National Origin Hatred

The Federal Bureau of Investigation's annual *Hate Crime Statistics* lists crimes caused by xenophobia in a category titled ethnicity/national origin. *Ethnicity* refers to a person's membership in a group from a particular country or region of the world who share a common language, customs, and beliefs. For example, Latinos speak Spanish, are mostly Roman Catholic, and have similar cultural traditions. *National origin* refers to someone's native country. Hate crimes against such immigrants are motivated by the fear that they will weaken or alter their new homeland economically, politically, or culturally.

In 2005 the FBI reported 944 such hate crimes. The incidents involved 1,144 criminal offenses, 1,228 victims, and 1,115 known offenders. More than half of the victims—722—were Latino. Many other victims were Arab or people who appeared to be Arab. They were targeted because the terrorists who attacked the United States on September 11, 2001, were Arab, an ethnic group from Middle Eastern countries such as Saudi Arabia, Syria, and Iraq. The terrorists were also Muslims, which sparked many religious hate crimes. Not all Arabs, however, are Muslim, and not all Middle Easterners are Arab.

Despite the FBI's statistics, it is believed that many more hate crimes were committed against Latinos, but these crimes were not officially reported. Many Latinos do not report such offenses

In 2005 more than half of the victims of hate crimes against immigrants were Latino.

because they or members of their family are illegal immigrants, and they fear they could be deported. It is this controversy over the legal status of immigrants, particularly Latinos, that has ignited most of these hate crimes.

Mexicans Are "Invaders"

In August 2006 the Office of Immigration Statistics estimated that more than half of the 11 million people living illegally in the United States, about 6 million, were from Mexico. This realization raised legitimate concerns about illegal immigration, such as the ease with which Mexicans could enter the United States and the social cost of caring for them. Anger over this emotional issue combined with ethnic hatred to ignite a wave of violence against Mexicans and other Latinos.

SENSELESS ACTS

"The acts alleged in this indictment are senseless. Individuals were assaulted merely because of the color of their skin and ethnic background."

Federal Bureau of Investigation special agent Tim Fuhrman on hate-crime charges filed against three men who attacked a Latino. Quoted in Geoffrey Fattah and Ben Winslow, "Hate-Crimes Crackdown," *Salt Lake City Deseret Morning News,* June 10, 2006, p. B1.

At a public park in Tucson, Arizona, on May 6, 2006, people were celebrating Cinco de Mayo, which commemorates the victory of Mexican forces over occupying French troops in 1862. The peaceful gathering was interrupted by members of the Border Guardians, an anti-immigration group led by Roy Warden. With a pistol strapped to his leg, Warden told the gathered Latinos, "Listen up, Mexican invaders. We will not permit you, the ignorant, the savage, the unwashed, to overrun us. [If] any invader tries to take this land from us we will wash this land and nurture our soil with oceans of their blood!" Warden later sent a threatening e-mail to Isabel Garcia, a Tucson public defender who heads Derechos Humanos, a Latino human-rights group. The email was titled, "Warden to Isabel Garcia: I will blow your freaking head off!"[59]

That was one of many Internet threats against Latinos. In June 2006 a group called Save Our States posted a press release on its

Web site "inviting people to go to a day-laborer hiring site in Redondo Beach and to bring their baseball bats."[60] Because many Latinos work as day laborers, it was considered an invitation to beat them. Also available on the Internet were hateful video games that could be downloaded and played. In one game, titled *Border Patrol*, players shot at Mexicans trying to cross the border into the United States.

Ethnic hatred also flares into physical violence. In April 2006 two teenagers in Houston, Texas, were charged with aggravated sexual assault for attacking a seventeen-year-old Latino boy. In describing the brutal attack, Harris County prosecutor Mike Trent says, "It looks like they were really trying to kill him and torture him anyway they could."[61] The teens burned their victim's neck with cigarettes, kicked his head, and slashed his chest with a knife because they thought he had kissed a white girl. The female student was actually Hispanic.

In the United States the controversy over the legal status of immigrants, particularly Mexicans and other Latinos, has ignited a wave of hate crimes against these groups.

Seeing Only a Turban and a Beard

Mistaken identity has played a part in many hate crimes following the September 11, 2001, attacks on New York and Washington, D.C. In seeking revenge on Muslim Arab terrorists, some perpetrators accidentally targeted non-Muslim Arab Americans as well as people from several countries who were neither Arab nor Muslim. On September 23, 2001, an arson fire at St. George's Assyrian Church in Chicago caused $250,000 in damage. Although the church's members are from Arab countries, they are Christians. Father Charles Klutz says, "The attack against our church is an attack against everyone, regardless of your ethnic background or your religion."[62]

A CASE OF MISDIRECTED HATE

"It's sadly not unknown for Sikh individuals to be targeted as victims of hate crimes by people who perceive them as a quote-unquote terrorist or a quote-unquote Muslim extremist. This crime seems to fit that horrible pattern."

Prosecutor Jay Boyarsky commenting on the slaying of Iqbal Singh, a Sikh killed by a neighbor. Quoted in John Cot, "Hate Crime Alleged in Stabbing of Sikh," *San Francisco Chronicle*, August 2, 2006, p. B10.

Five years later, Christian Arabs still feared attacks from people who mistakenly believed they were Muslim. Dany Fahmy lives in Washington State. Despite being Christian, Fahmy said in August 2006 that he knew he could be targeted for a hate crime because he has Arabic features. "No one could look at me and tell if I'm an Arabic Christian, an Arabic Southern Baptist, or an Arabic Shi'ite,"[63] he said. His family immigrated to the United States from Beirut, Lebanon, so that his father, a Southern Baptist minister, could work with Arab Christians.

People from countries such as India and Pakistan, who are neither Arab nor Muslim, have been attacked by hate-crime predators who thought they were. On September 15, 2001, Frank Roque shot to death Balbir Singh Sodhi in Mesa, Arizona. Roque wanted to kill an Arab Muslim in revenge for the attacks by al Qaeda. Sodhi, however, was from India and was a member of the Sikh reli-

Since the September 11, 2001, terrorist attacks, an increasing number of hate crimes have been committed against people who look like they are Arab or Muslim, but who—such as these members of the Sikh religion—in fact, are neither.

gion. Roque thought he was an Arab Muslim because he wore a turban and had a long beard, both of which are Sikh cultural traditions. However, these features made Sodhi look like Roque's stereotyped conception of Arab Muslims, who wear head coverings, called kaffiyehs, and often have beards.

Many other cases of mistaken identity have occurred. In 2003 several Sikh cab drivers in the San Francisco area were shot to death. Baljit Singh explains why his fellow Sikhs were being targeted: "They just see the turban and the beard and they hate us."[64] And it happened again on July 30, 2006, when Iqbal Singh, age forty, was shot to death in Santa Clara, California, by a neighbor who thought the Sikh was a Muslim.

Attacking the Most Vulnerable

The same hatred that incited the death of Singh has been responsible for numerous hate crimes against people with mental and

Afraid to Report a Hate Crime

It is believed that many more hate crimes are committed against people with disabilities than are reported. Veronica Robertson, an activist for the disabled community in Chicago, claims that one reason why many people with disabilities do not report such offenses is because they are afraid of their attackers. "They're scared that the perpetrator will go after them again," Robertson says. In Kathi Wolfe's article "Bashing the Disabled," Robertson recounts how this fear ruined the life of one disabled person:

He's a quadriplegic in his mid-thirties who lives in subsidized housing on the north side of Chicago. Every time he goes out-side, the same guy beats him up. While he's beating him, he says, "I don't want you out here, you crip-ple. I don't like your kind. You people bring down the commu-nity." This man is terrified of leav-ing his apartment building because he knows he'll be beaten and ver-bally abused. And he's too fright-ened to report the hate crime because the perpetrator has told him, "If you tell anyone about this, I'll beat your [profanity deleted]."

Kathi Wolfe, "Bashing the Disabled: The New Hate Crime," *Progressive*, November 1995, p. 8.

physical disabilities. Just as Singh's killer hated him on sight, some people feel an immediate hatred when they see people with dis-abilities. According to the FBI, which tallies hate crimes commit-ted against people with disabilities, in 2004 fifty-seven such incidents occurred. Thirty-four of these hate crimes involved peo-ple with mental disabilities, and twenty-three involved people with physical disabilities; a total of seventy-three victims were involved. Kathi Wolfe, who is blind, knows that some people hate the sight of the disabled. She encountered this unreasoning hatred once while entering a subway station in Washington, D.C. Wolfe recalls:

"Move, blind lady," a man hissed at me as he twisted my arm and grabbed my cane. He threw my cane down the escalator. He spat on me and growled, "You people be-long in concentration camps." I knew that some people dislike those of us with disabilities, but before this encounter at the subway, I had no idea that this hostility could take the form of such rabid hatred.[65]

Mark Sherry also has firsthand knowledge of the prejudices faced by the disabled. His life changed drastically in 1992 after he was run over by a car in his native Australia. In addition to serious internal injuries, Sherry suffered a brain injury that left him disabled by recurring epileptic seizures. As a result, Sherry dedicated his life to researching issues affecting people with disabilities, such as hate crimes. One disturbing fact that Sherry has learned is how much some people hate the disabled. He says this hatred is evident in many ways, from angry stares directed at disabled people in public places to Internet sites that express revulsion for them. Sherry, who has taught at several U.S. universities, wants the world to understand this hatred: "I want people to recognize that hate exists toward disabled people. Often people's assumption is that people have condescension or pity [for the disabled]. But nondisabled people do not want to acknowledge that they hate disabled people, that they hate our difference."[66]

All Walks of Life, a rights group for disabled people in Houston, Texas, also works to educate the public about issues affecting people with disabilities. The group explains that physical problems make some disabled people easy prey for hate-crime perpetrators:

> The main cause of violence to people with disabilities is vulnerability. Vulnerability to predators who take advantage of people with developmental, mental and physical disabilities. They are not as able at defending, resisting and/or reporting a physical attack as their nondisabled peers because of their disability.[67]

An example of how this vulnerability works against the disabled occurred in Milltown, New Jersey. On January 30, 1999, Eric Krochmaluk, who is cognitively disabled, accepted an invitation from acquaintances who told him, "Come to a party, you might meet a nice girl."[68] At the party, eight men and women kept Krochmaluk prisoner while they shaved his eyebrows, beat him, burned him with a cigarette, and choked him. Krochmaluk went

Physical and mental problems make some disabled people easy targets for hate crime perpetrators.

to the party even though the same people had abused him in the past; because of his disability, he was unable to comprehend that they might hurt him again.

A similar incident happened to Jean Parker, a past executive director of the Colorado Cross-Disability Coalition, who is blind. She was attacked while waiting for a bus in Denver. She recalls, "Someone silently approached and deliberately kicked my guide dog in the kidneys."[69] Parker could not see the attacker, which meant she had no way to stop the assault.

Parker's lack of sight also meant that she had no way to identify the hate-crime perpetrator. Mark Sherry claims the trouble that disabled people have in reporting hate crimes is one reason why thousands of such offenses are never reported. "If you believe [FBI statistics], disabled people have less than one in a million chance of experiencing a hate crime. I think that's pure fantasy,"[70] he says. Sherry's claim is based on the fact that even though there are more than 53 million disabled people in the United States, only a handful of crimes against them are reported each year. He believes that as many as ten thousand hate crimes are actually committed annually against the disabled.

Not a Protected Class

Although at least some hate crimes against the disabled are reported, acts of violence against another group—the homeless—are not even considered hate crimes by the federal government or most states. Many people, however, believe they should be because the homeless are regularly targeted for offenses that are usually considered hate crimes. The National Coalition for the Homeless (NCH) reports that in 2005 there were 86 attacks against homeless people, including 13 that resulted in death. That was a decrease from 105 attacks in 2004, when twenty-five people were

A Catalog of Homeless Hate Crimes

In June 2006 the National Coalition for the Homeless issued a report on violence against the homeless that occurred the previous year. This is an excerpt from that report:

In February [2005], Maria Catherine King, a homeless woman of less than 100 pounds who had been struggling with mental illness, was brutally beaten and killed in Berkeley, California. The suspects were two 18-year-old males. [In] May, in Holly Hill, Florida, five teenagers charged with killing a homeless man said they did it "for fun" because they "needed something to do." The five teens left the scene and re-turned numerous times to beat Michael Roberts, 53, with their fists, tree branches, and a large log. In August, in Los Angeles, two 19-year-old men [took] to the streets, hitting sleeping homeless people with aluminum baseball bats and leaving an elderly man in critical condition. Sadly, these gruesome accounts are just a few of many that demonstrate the hate/violence faced by people experiencing homelessness each year.

National Coalition for the Homeless, "Hate, Violence, and Death on Main Street USA: A Report on Hate Crimes and Violence Against People Experiencing Homelessness, 2005," June 2006. www.nationalhomeless.org/getinvolved/projects/hatecrimes/index.html.

killed, including forty-nine-year-old Rex Baum, who was beaten to death in Milwaukee, Wisconsin, with rocks, a flashlight, and a pipe.

Several homeless people die each year when they are intentionally set on fire. On March 5, 2006, one homeless man escaped such a death in Boston after he was doused with lighter fluid and set ablaze in a city park. "I was screaming. I could feel my skin melting. I just kicked off my shoes and shucked my pants off. Oh, it hurt,"[71] says the man, who suffered second-degree burns on his left leg. Michael Stoops of the NCH says that arson and baseball-bat beatings "are the two most common forms" of violence against the homeless. Stoops contends, "If this were happening to anyone else, there'd be an uproar. It really baffles me."[72]

Because of their living situations, homeless people are particularly vulnerable to attacks. Yet violence against the homeless is not classified as a hate crime by the federal government or most states.

Crimes against the homeless are similar to those against the disabled in an important way: Members of both groups are easy to attack. Karen LaFrazia is executive director of St. Francis House, a homeless shelter in Boston. "Homeless people by virtue of their living situation are very vulnerable. They are easy targets for angry people,"[73] she says. According to LaFrazia, every week a few of the people she cares for, most of them women, report they have been attacked.

HARASSING THOSE WHO CANNOT FIGHT BACK

"Regardless of [their] cognitive disability people do not deserve to have signs pointed at them, making fun of them, scaring them, harassing them."

Fraser Nelson, executive director of the Disability Law Center, commenting on a sign someone hung in Nephi, Utah, referring to a thirteen-year-old boy. The sign read, "Caution, Retards in Area." Quoted in Sam Penrod, "Derogatory Sign Offends Family in Nephi," *Salt Lake City Deseret News,* July 2006, p. B4.

To prevent such attacks, it is important to gain an understanding of the people who commit hate crimes. For some individuals, differences in race, religion, ethnicity, ability, and sexual orientation can bring about feelings of fear and hatred, which often erupt in violence. For others, prejudices have been instilled since childhood and are difficult to overcome. Recognizing the characteristics common to all hate-crime perpetrators is an important step in combating hate crimes.

THE PERPETRATORS OF HATE CRIMES

When John William King chained James Byrd Jr. to the rear of a truck and dragged him to his death over a bumpy rural road in Jasper, Texas, on June 7, 1998, he had another motive in addition to racial hatred. (King and two accomplices, Shawn Allen Berry and Lawrence Russell Brewer, were convicted of Byrd's death in separate trials.) A witness claimed during King's 1999 murder trial that King killed Byrd to impress the Ku Klux Klan. King hoped to sufficiently impress the racist organization so that it would allow a group he was forming, called the Texas Rebel Soldiers, to join the KKK. William Hoover testified that when he and King were in prison together, King told him that killing a black person was a good way to win such acceptance. "To help new recruits get initiated, take somebody out and kill them,"[74] Hoover recalls King stating.

Byrd's slaying was only one of thousands that have been linked to the nation's oldest and most infamous hate group. Some 150 years after it was founded, the KKK is still promoting racial, religious, and ethnic hatred in the twenty-first century. It is, however, only one of scores of such groups responsible for hate crimes. Some organizations pattern themselves after Nazi leader Adolf Hitler, hating blacks, Jews, and homosexuals; others advocate ethnic violence against Latinos and Arabs; and many persecute people because of their sexual orientation.

Not all people who commit hate crimes belong to these groups. Yet such organizations often sway hate-crime perpetrators with their hateful philosophies. Jacob Robida used a gun and hatchet in February 2006 to wound three gay men in New Bedford, Massachusetts. Robida did not belong to a neo-Nazi group, but he openly admired their views and had a tattoo of a swastika. He also used the Nazi symbol to decorate a Myspace.com Web site, in which he wrote, "I'm interested in death, destruction, chaos, filth and greed."[75] Robida had something else in common with many hate-crime perpetrators—he was young, just eighteen years old. A West Virginia University study shows that between 1995 and 2000, 20.7 percent of hate-crime perpetrators were younger than eighteen, and 18.6 percent were aged eighteen to twenty-four.

Racism as Holy War

The two most common factors that hate-crime perpetrators share are youth and a link to a hate group. Due to their success in appealing to young people, hate groups experienced a surge in membership during the early twenty-first century. The Southern Poverty Law Center, which was founded in 1971 to promote civil rights, tracks the activities of hate groups through its Intelligence

The Ku Klux Klan, whose members don white robes and masks at rallies, is the oldest hate group in the United States.

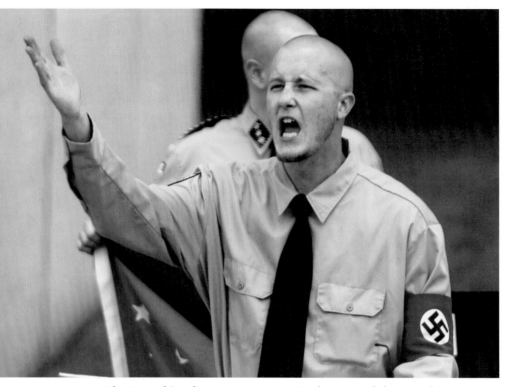

The National Socialist Movement, a neo-Nazi hate group, believes in white supremacy.

Project. (The project was originally called Klanwatch because it began by monitoring KKK violence.) The center reports that in 2005 there were 803 active U.S. hate groups; that figure represented a 5 percent increase in such groups from 2004 and a 33 percent jump since 2000. The groups all spread hate speech; many of them advocate violence against blacks, Jews, Muslims, Latinos, and gays; and a few commit hate crimes.

Most hate groups fit into three main categories: neo-Nazis, such as the National Socialist Movement (NSM); the KKK and other racist groups; and Skinheads, whose members are mainly young people. These organizations all believe in white supremacy. Typical of their racial beliefs are those of the Creativity Movement, which was once known as the World Church of the Creator. The Creativity Movement's motto is "RaHoWa," short for "Racial Holy War." Its members claim that nonwhites are "sub-human" and "natural" enemies of whites, and the group's goal is "survival, expansion, and advancement of [the] White Race exclusively."[76]

The KKK and the NSM are two of the biggest hate groups and have been active for many years. In 2005 the KKK had an estimated 179 groups with names like the Imperial Klans of America and the Mystic Knights; the National Socialists boasted 59 chapters. There are no solid membership figures for these groups, but it is believed that they have thousands of members in the United States. In the early twenty-first century, organizations such as the Border Guardians and Texas Minutemen were created to oppose illegal immigration. Although illegal immigration is a legitimate issue, some people have joined these groups because they hate all Mexicans, even those who are U.S. citizens.

PLANTING THE SEEDS OF HATRED

"Not everybody who is receptive contacts us. Some people will just start visiting our website and listening to our radio broadcasts. Some will become active supporters of our cause; others will become passive supporters."

A leader of the white supremacist Arizona National Vanguard commenting on what people do after they receive a flyer from the group. Quoted in Chip Berlet, "The Hard Edge of Hatred," *Nation*, August 15, 2006. www.thenation.com/doc/20060828/new_nativism.

There are also many small hate groups. One is Westboro Baptist Church in Topeka, Kansas, whose members hate homosexuals because they believe the Bible condemns them. In protests at the funerals of soldiers killed in the Iraq War, members carried signs that read, "Thank God for Dead Soldiers." They claimed the deaths were a punishment from God because the United States tolerates homosexuality. The protests were universally condemned because they added to the suffering of the families and friends who were already mourning the deaths of loved ones.

How Hate Groups Attract Members

Whereas Westboro has only a few members, hate groups such as the KKK and the NSM have much larger memberships, in part because they have sophisticated ways to attract followers. One strategy is to stage controversial events to get media coverage. On

A Hate Group "Juggernaut"

In the early years of the twenty-first century, one of the largest and fastest-growing hate groups was the neo-Nazi National Socialist Movement (NSM). In 2006 the Southern Poverty Law Center's *Intelligence Report* declared that the group, "once a forgotten bit player on the fringe of the American Radical Right, is building a juggernaut." The *Intelligence Report* said it was winning new members with aggressive, confrontational tactics:

> The membership of the NSM is generally younger than other neo-Nazi groups [and] its tactics and image [are] far more crudely aggressive. At a summer 2002 rally in Topeka, Kansas, when 21 NSM members faced off with hundreds of anti-Nazi demonstrators, [Jeff] Schoep waved a noose. More recently, on Martin Luther King Day 2006, members of NSM's three Ohio units protested outside a King memorial ceremony in Troy, Ohio. "They had a long-winded prayer about that filthy [King] and I kept interrupting them with loud comments about Church's Fried Chicken and how the collard greens was gettin' cold," reported NSM Ohio leader Mann Mark Martin, who recently defected to NSM from White Revolution. "Ahhh . . . I love free speech."

Intelligence Report, "The National Socialist Movement, Once a Forgotten Bit Player on the Fringe of the American Radical Right, Is Building a Juggernaut," Spring 2006. www.splcenter.org/intel/intelreport/article.jsp?aid=617.

October 16, 2005, the NSM held a rally in a black section of Toledo, Ohio, because it hoped its presence would incite a violent counterprotest. When blacks and other people who opposed the group's racist creed attacked NSM members, police had to arrest sixty people to protect the neo-Nazis. Millions of people read stories or viewed television coverage of the event, which helped make people aware of the group. NSM leader Jeff Schoep was also able to claim in such stories that the violence proved his group's racist contention that blacks are savage.

The Stormfront White Nationalist Community pioneered one of the most powerful tactics to win converts. In March 1995 the group started the first Internet hate site. The site was created by Don Black, a former Klansman who believed the new technology would allow hate groups to easily communicate with many more people. Today Stormfront is no longer alone in disseminating hatred. In 2005 the *Intelligence Report* counted 524 hate sites, a 12 percent increase from 468 a year earlier. Mark Potok, the magazine's editor, once explained that the "veritable explosion of hate sites" since Stormfront began is due to the ease with which the Internet allows them to promote their ideas:

> A few years ago, a Klansman needed to put out substantial effort and money to produce and distribute a shoddy pamphlet that might reach a few hundred people. Today, with a $500 computer and negligible other costs, that same Klansman can put up a slickly produced Web site with a potential audience in the millions.[77]

Teenagers and young adults often visit hate sites out of idle curiosity about such groups or because of a fascination with the symbols they use, such as the Nazi swastika. Hate groups welcome

To gain publicity for their group, typically via news coverage, the National Socialist Movement often holds marches in predominantly black or Jewish neighborhoods so as to incite large groups of counterprotesters.

young people, who are often too naive to understand that the racist and hateful messages their sites present are based on lies and faulty stereotypes, such as that all blacks are promiscuous or all Jewish people are greedy.

HOW MUCH FORCE IS TOO MUCH?

"This is great! They got it on tape! Now we'll have a live, in-the-field film to show police recruits. It can be a real life example of how to use escalating force properly."

Los Angeles police sergeant Stacey Koon commenting on the videotape that caught him and other officers beating Rodney King in 1991. Quoted in Douglas O. Linder, "Famous Trials: The Rodney King Beating (LAPD Officers') Trial: In Their Own Words," University of Missouri-Kansas City. www.law.umkc.edu/faculty/projects/ftrials/lapd/kingownwords. html.

Hate groups also try to recruit young people with "white power" music. Panzerfaust Records in South St. Paul, Minnesota, is one of several companies that produce hard-rock music with white-supremacy messages. Groups that sing the songs also perform at rallies. Prussian Blue is the duo of fraternal twins Lynx and Lamb Gaede. In 2005 the fourteen-year-old blonde, blue-eyed sisters appeared at rallies for Kulturkampf, a neo-Nazi anti-immigrant group. They once claimed in an interview that the most pressing problem today is "not having enough white babies born to replace ourselves and generally not having good-quality white people being born."[78] Their songs have titles like "Aryan Man Awake"; *Aryan* is a reference to Hitler's alleged master race of whites.

Jonathan Bernstein of the Anti-Defamation League says such tactics have helped lure young people to hate groups. He says many young people become Skinheads after being exposed to such racist commentary. According to Bernstein, "Skinheads are often the foot soldiers for the leaders of the hate movement. They are responsible for much of the hate violence."[79]

Youthful Perpetrators

Skinheads are the most well-known group of young hate-crime perpetrators. Members of such groups have many things in common, as the Federal Bureau of Investigation has learned. The FBI conducted a seven-year study of racist Skinhead groups like California's Nazi Low Riders. The study showed that most members are uneducated white males between thirteen and twenty-four years of age who are unemployed or have low-paying jobs, and their main form of recreation is getting drunk and taking drugs. When they are high, the Skinheads often go looking for people to beat up. Because they have learned from their families, friends, or society to hate people who are different, their victims are usually blacks, Latinos, Jews, and gays. Hate-crime expert Jack Levin explains the psychological rage that fuels such violence: "They're not doing well in school, they see little hope for their future, but in hate they feel special, they feel important at someone else's [their victim's] expense. They're bored, they're idle and they're looking to

A Typical Racist Skinhead

Between 1992 and 1999, the Federal Bureau of Investigation conducted an investigation of Skinhead gangs in California to learn more about the violent youths who often commit hate crimes. FBI agents interviewed hundreds of Skinheads for the study. One of the Skinheads they interviewed belonged to the Nazi Low Riders in Lancaster, California. Gang members prowled the streets of Lancaster in search of minorities, who they would beat and sometimes stab; they were also linked to the murder of an African American. The following comments, excerpted from the March 2003 *FBI Law Enforcement Bulletin,* are from a fifteen-year-old who was considered a typical gang member:

I dropped out of school in the eighth grade, but I stopped learning midway through the sixth grade. I covered my body with hate tattoos. I couldn't get a good job if I wanted to. No one would hire me. Once, I tried to get a job at a fast food restaurant, but the manager refused to hire me because the restaurant served multiracial customers. If I quit being a skinhead, I have nothing. I am nothing. I have no choice but to be a skinhead. I expect to die a young, violent death.

Joe Navarro and John R. Schafer, "The Seven-Stage Hate Model: The Psychopathology of Hate Groups," *FBI Law Enforcement Bulletin,* March 2003, p. 5.

Skinheads are the most well-known group of young hate-crime perpetrators. Hate groups aim to recruit young people to continually populate their rosters.

feel a little excitement and this is how they choose to do it."[80]

Skinheads are usually from poor families in big cities. But Levin notes that, starting in the 1990s, an increasing number of youthful hate-crime perpetrators have come from middle-class and affluent suburban areas. Levin believes this increase coincides with an increase of minority families moving into the suburbs. He claims, "These [suburban] kids aren't prepared for people who are different. They see them as a threat. They come home in the afternoon to their empty houses, log onto the Internet, visit hate sites, chat rooms, bulletin boards and get ideas."[81]

An example of hate crimes committed by such young people occurred in Alabama in February 2006 when three Birmingham-Southern College students were arrested in a string of arson fires at churches, several of them with black congregations. Initially, officials believed the fires were set by the KKK or other hate groups. "This is just so hard to believe. My profile on these suspects is shot all to heck and back,"[82] state fire marshal Richard W. Montgomery said when he learned the students were responsible for the fires. Montgomery was shocked because the students, one of them the son of a doctor, were so unlike most of the people who have committed such crimes in the past.

Law Enforcement Hate Crimes

Although teens and young adults are responsible for nearly half of all hate crimes, many older adults also commit them. Sometimes the people expected to uphold the law are the ones committing the crimes. There have been a few high-profile cases of police officers committing hate crimes, and some studies suggest that this is a problem that often goes unreported. One group often targeted by law enforcement officials consists of lesbian, gay, bisexual, and transgender people. In 2005 Amnesty International (AI), which tracks human-rights violations worldwide, issued a 159-page report on such hate crimes. AI spokesman William F. Schulz says, "Across the country [such people] endure the injustices of discrimination, entrapment and verbal abuse, as well as brutal beatings and sexual assault at the hands of those responsible for protecting them—the police."[83] One incident cited in the AI report involved the way New York officers treated a transgender man whom they had arrested. According to the report, after placing him in a cell for women, "officers walked past him repeatedly, mocking his name and asking, 'What is this thing?'"[84]

Other incidents that raise concern are those in which white police officers use excessive force when arresting African Americans. One infamous case involved Rodney King, who, on March 3, 1991, was brutally attacked by Los Angeles police

Though bound to uphold the law, police officers are not exempt from committing hate crimes. Groups such as the Los Angeles Coalition for Justice and Peace to End Police Brutality, pictured, monitor alleged cases of police brutality.

officers when they arrested him for speeding. The officers claimed that King was resisting arrest and that they were only doing what was necessary to subdue him. The incident, however, had been videotaped by a bystander. When it was shown on television, it created a firestorm of controversy about police brutality. In 1992, when the four officers charged with using excessive force to subdue King were found not guilty, Los Angeles blacks were so angry that they erupted in one of the city's worst riots.

The King beating was the first of several videotaped incidents involving white officers who appeared to use excessive force when arresting African Americans. Retired teacher Robert Davis, age sixty-four, was savagely beaten in New Orleans, Louisiana, on October 8, 2005, by white police officers who arrested him for public drunkenness. The police claimed that race was not a factor and that Davis resisted arrest. The charge was later dropped, and Davis claimed, "I haven't had a drink in 25 years."[85] Davis was in New Orleans to check on property his family owned that had been damaged a month earlier by Hurricane Katrina. Two of the police officers involved were fired, and a third officer was suspended for his actions.

DEFENDING AMERICA BY PROMOTING HATE

"This is a symbolic act. We felt that when people are taking to the streets, it was an assertion of Mexican sovereignty. Today we are defending American sovereignty."

Roy Warden, leader of the Border Guardians, explaining why he burned a Mexican flag to protest illegal immigration. Quoted in Levi J. Long, "Mexican-Flag Burners Plan More Protests," *Arizona Daily Star,* April 10, 2006, p. B1.

Some law enforcement officials belong to racist groups. The Nebraska State Patrol fired Robert Henderson on June 26, 2006, because he was a member of the Ku Klux Klan. Nebraska attorney general Jon Bruning said at the time, "We don't want the agency destroyed by a racist like Bob Henderson."[86] On August 18, 2006, however, a state labor arbitrator reinstated Henderson after ruling that the dismissal violated the trooper's constitutional right to free speech.

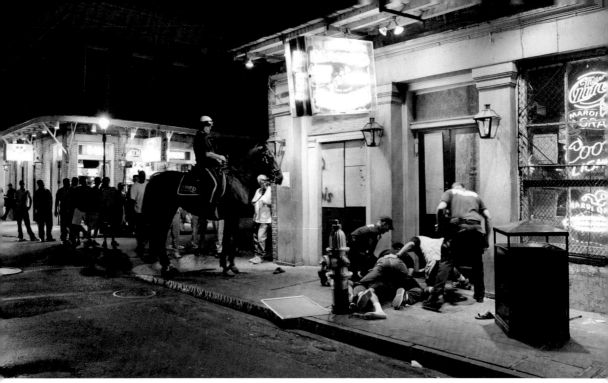

When sixty-four-year-old Robert Davis was arrested for public drunkeness, pictured, some felt it was a case of excessive police force; others believed the police acted within the law.

"You Are Cowards"

Thus, there are many types of people who commit hate crimes, but some people claim these perpetrators all have one thing in common: They are cowards. On July 29, 2006, three men used baseball bats and knives to assault five gay men in San Diego, California. Two days later, when San Diego mayor Jerry Sanders promised to find the men, he said, "I have a few choice words for the criminals who committed this vicious attack—you are cowards."[87] Even though the gay men outnumbered their attackers, Sanders labeled them cowards because their victims were unarmed. Studies have shown, however, that perpetrators usually outnumber victims in hate crimes. That is why many people accuse them of cowardice.

An example of this was evident in Utah on November 3, 2005, when U.S. attorney Paul Warner charged three whites with beating a black man. In announcing the charges, Warner questioned their bravery: "These people are cowards. They attack at night, they attack in the dark, they attack in overwhelming numbers."[88]

CHAPTER 7

FIGHTING HATE CRIMES

Thousands of hate crimes are committed every year. Because hate crimes affect not only victims but also everyone in the communities in which they occur, state and local governments, private groups, and individuals have all banded together to stop them.

Governments can outlaw some types of hate crime by passing new laws. On June 15, 2006, New York governor George Pataki signed into law a bill that makes burning crosses or putting swastikas on public buildings a felony crime. "Malicious acts that incite fear or promote hatred and intolerance have no place in the Empire State or anywhere in this great nation,"[89] Pataki says.

Private organizations often work to stop hateful acts. When the National Socialist Movement (NSM) announced it would hold a rally on July 3, 2006, in Olympia, Washington, a group called Unity in the Community was formed to oppose it. The group was a broad-based coalition of faith groups, institutions, and schools that wanted to fight racism. So many people showed up to protest the NSM rally that protesters outnumbered the neo-Nazis five hundred to thirteen. Bryn Houghton, a resident of Olympia, came dressed as a clown with a fake mustache like the one Adolf Hitler wore. Houghton said protesters made so much noise that "you couldn't hear them [the neo-Nazis]."[90]

Even individuals can fight hate crime. Karen Zielinski, a Franciscan nun who has multiple sclerosis, advises the disabled on how to protect themselves. "Although some of us might not be able to enroll in a self-defense class, all of us can arm ourselves with one type of critical self-defense: common sense,"[91] she writes. One of her tips is to carry personal alarm devices that people can use to call for help if they are attacked.

Laws to Stop Hate Crimes

Although federal and state laws like the one Governor Pataki signed in 2006 can outlaw hate crimes, they can never end the hatred that causes them. Such laws, however, can sufficiently punish perpetrators to make people think twice before committing such offenses. In 2006 every state except Wyoming had laws against hate crimes. Some states have created new criminal offenses for hate crimes, and others have simply increased penalties for existing crimes in which the offenses can also be considered hate crimes. Both types of laws result in longer jail or prison sentences for perpetrators.

State officials believe harsher punishment is necessary for hate crimes because they affect society as a whole. On July 17, 2006, Nicholas Minucci was sentenced to fifteen years in prison for beating Glenn Moore, a black man walking through his Howard Beach, New York, neighborhood. He also stole Moore's shoes. Minucci's sentence was nearly twice the state-allowed minimum for the charges of robbery and assault if the offense had not been a hate

Hate crimes hurt entire communities, not just the victims of the crime. Each year thousands of concerned citizens do their part to combat hate.

crime. Queens district attorney Richard Brown explains why the longer prison term was justified: "The sentence reflect[s] an understanding of the fact that when Nicholas Minucci picked up that aluminum baseball bat on June 29 of last year in Howard Beach, he raised that bat against not only Glenn Moore, but against every other resident of this city."[92]

Most state laws add extra punishment for hate crimes motivated by race, religion, or ethnicity. In 2006, however, many states did not include sexual orientation as a hate-crime motivation, and none covered homeless people. The lack of protection for the homeless was highlighted in Fort Lauderdale, Florida, on January 12, 2006, when three teenagers were charged with first-degree murder after they used a baseball bat to kill Norris Gaynor, who was homeless. The attack, which was recorded by a surveillance camera, gained worldwide attention when it was shown on televi-

As of 2006 every state except Wyoming had laws against hate crimes. Here, Hawaii lieutenant governor Mazie Hirono signs Hawaii's hate crime bill into law in 2001.

The Importance of Community Response

When a hate crime occurs, one of the most powerful things government and community leaders can do is condemn the offense. Hate-crime experts Jack Levin and Jack McDevitt explain why:

> First of all, community leaders must speak out condemning the attack. This is important because it sends two essential messages: to the victims, that local residents want them to remain members of that community and, to the offenders, that most people in the community do not support their illegal behavior. Interviews with hate crime offenders indicate that they frequently believe that most of the community shares their desire to eliminate the "outsider." The offenders often see themselves as heroes or at least as "cool" in the eyes of their friends, because they have the courage to act on what they believe to be commonly held beliefs. Public statements by local community leaders challenge this idea and send a message to offenders that their actions are not supported.

Jack Levin and Jack McDevitt, "Hate Crimes," Brudnick Center on Violence and Conflict, Northeastern University. www.violence.neu.edu/publication4.html.

sion newscasts. Gaynor's brutal slaying made many people believe such offenses should be considered hate crimes.

In 2006 many states were considering expanding hate-crime coverage to include crimes involving sexual orientation and the homeless. This was important because the federal role in prosecuting hate crimes is limited. Federal charges can be filed under a 1969 civil rights law only if the act occurs during a few protected activities, such as voting, going to school, using public facilities, or working. The U.S. government does not prosecute many hate crimes because it believes that is the role of states. However, the federal government fights hate crimes by compiling hate-crime statistics, educating the public on hate crimes, and assisting hate-crime victims through agencies such as the U. S. Department of Justice's Community Relations Service.

Local governments also fight hate crimes. Fairfax, Virginia, officials print and distribute a brochure in six languages so that hate-crime victims who do not speak English will know how to report offenses. Likewise, on May 17, 2006, Boulder, Colorado, became the first city in the nation to authorize a hate-crime hotline. That telephone service was similar to many that private groups were already operating in many cities.

Monitoring and Fighting Hate

In addition to telephone hotlines, private organizations use a variety of methods and approaches to combat hate crimes. The Southern Poverty Law Center has been battling hate crimes since it was founded in 1971 to help blacks gain their civil rights. The SPLC monitors hate-crime activity; publicizes offenses in its quarterly magazine, the *Intelligence Report;* and uses legal action to cripple hate groups such as the Ku Klux Klan. In 1988 the SPLC won nearly $1 million in damages for eleven Georgia residents who had been attacked by members of the Invisible Empire Knights. Once one of the nation's largest and most violent KKK groups, the court decision left the Invisible Empire bankrupt and forced it to disband.

INTOLERANCE WILL NOT BE TOLERATED

"That is not what California stands for. The greatness of California is its rich diversity. Hate, racism and intolerance are never accepted in our public debates. I encourage all people to spread the good word of tolerance."

California governor Arnold Schwarzenegger commenting on hate threats against Mexican American public officials. Arnold Swarzenegger, "Governor Arnold Schwarzenegger's Remarks at Executive Order Signing for Crime Victim Advocate," Office of the Governor, April 24, 2006. www.gov.ca.gov/index.php/speech/160.

Another powerful hate-crime opponent is the Anti-Defamation League, which was founded in 1913. It has one of the most comprehensive and informative hate-crime Web sites (www.adl.org), and it monitors hate crimes through its many local offices. The ADL is one of many organizations that directly represent groups of people who are targeted for hate crimes. Other organizations include the American-Arab Anti-Discrimination Committee, the National Association for the Advancement of Colored People, the

A number of powerful anti-hate groups, such as Parents, Family, and Friends of Lesbians and Gays (PFLAG), are operating in the United States and elsewhere.

Asian American Legal Defense and Education Fund, and Parents and Friends of Lesbians and Gays. The ADL stresses, however, that everyone, not just possible victims, should be concerned about hate crimes:

> All Americans have a stake in an effective response to violent bigotry. Hate crimes demand a priority response because of their special emotional and psychological impact on the victim and the victim's community. [Such] incidents can damage the fabric of our society and fragment communities.[93]

One of those situations that could rip a community apart occurred in Seattle, Washington, on July 28, 2006, when Naveed Afzal Haq, a Muslim, killed fifty-eight-year-old Pamela Waechter and wounded several other Jewish people in a shooting rampage at the Jewish Federation of Greater Seattle. To heal the wound caused by the shooting, people of all faiths attended Waechter's July 31 funeral. "All lives are sacred,"[94] says Joy Carey, a Muslim. Andy Hoskins, an Episcopalian who attended, says, "I want people here [in the Jewish community] to know they have friends everywhere."[95] The show of support helped keep Seattle from being divided by hate.

Groups like the ADL, the Council on American-Islamic Relations, and LAMBDA—which mainly works with gay, lesbian, bisexual, and transgender people—also help victims cope with hate crimes. The groups help victims report hate crimes to the authorities, and many operate hate-crime hotlines. The groups also provide medical assistance and counseling for victims and advise them of their legal rights, such as what to do if their attacker is arrested and charged with the crime.

Educating People About Hate Crimes

One of the most important things that these groups do is to educate people about hate crimes. The ways in which they do this are almost limitless. Groups maintain Web sites, print publications, and sponsor speeches, lectures, and other public events. These

Often people of different backgrounds band together after a hate crime to help heal wounds in the community. Such was the case for this man after a shooting occurred at the Jewish Federation of Greater Seattle.

educational efforts are aimed not only at the general public but also at specialized audiences. The SPLC and the ADL both offer classes for law enforcement officials and teachers.

RESPECTING THOSE DIFFERENT FROM US

"This place is a place of worship. It's a place where people come to seek love and care. As a Muslim, I'm cleaning a Jewish building because my religion tells me: Respect every religion and religious place."

Saeed Shahzad, a Muslim, discussing why he was cleaning swastikas off Striar Jewish Community Center in Stoughton, Massachusetts. Quoted in Michael Levenson, "In Stoughton, They Join Hands to Wash Out Hate," *Boston Globe,* March 6, 2006, p. B2.

But Debra Chasnoff, executive director of the Respect for All Project, believes that students are the most important group that should be educated. Chasnoff, an Oscar-winning filmmaker, has directed several videos that explain hate crimes and show how people can become more tolerant of those who are different. In *Let's Get Real,* students who have been bullied because of race, religion, disabilities, or sexual orientation explain what happened to them and how they felt. The video includes interviews with student bullies who have realized that what they did was wrong. Chasnoff believes young people need to learn such lessons because school bullying is similar in many ways to hate crimes:

> We can no longer sit back and dismiss bullying as a rite of passage that all kids just have to live through. Unchecked bullying compromises student performance, damages physical and mental health, and perpetuates a cycle that can escalate to even greater, more brutal forms of violence, including hate crimes.[96]

Clinton Sipes could have benefited from hate-crime education when he was growing up. Although Sipes rejected white supremacy as an adult, he was a violent KKK member for many years. Sipes, who became a racist when he was fourteen years old, says, "I think if someone had come and told me, tried to teach me some things about people, I might have felt differently. I wouldn't have been so angry, but no one ever did."[97]

An educational program that has helped entire communities fight hate crimes is Not In Our Town (NIOT). In 1993 in Billings, Montana, white supremacists desecrated a Jewish cemetery, painted swastikas on a Native American family's house, and broke a window in the home of a family displaying a menorah, a Jewish religious symbol. The hate spree lasted several weeks and spurred city officials and community groups to fight back in a collective effort that became known as "Not In Our Town." A labor union painted over the swastikas, and civic organizations staged marches and protests against racism. When the *Billings Gazette* printed pictures of paper menorahs, ten thousand people of all faiths displayed them in their windows to show their unity with Jews.

How Young People Can Fight Hate Crimes

The National Youth Violence Prevention Resource Center Web site has information on hate crimes. Here are some suggestions on how young people can try to stop hate crimes:

Start with yourself. Try to broaden your social circle to include others who are different from you. Be mindful of your language—avoid stereotypical remarks and challenge those made by others. Speak out against jokes and slurs that target people or groups. Silence sends a message that you are in agreement. It is not enough to refuse to laugh.

Read books about diverse cultures, traditions, and lifestyles in our society. . . .

Talk with your friends, parents, and school staff about how you and your classmates can respond to hateful attitudes and behaviors. . . . Research and find out about hate crimes that have occurred in your community and what was done to respond to them. Identify any hate groups active in your community. . . .

Join an existing group that is promoting tolerance in your school or community, or launch your own effort. Join with other students to create anti-hate policies and programs in your school.

National Youth Violence Prevention Resource Center, "What You Can Do." www.safeyouth.org/scripts/teens/hate.asp.

Educating children about tolerance is the best way to stop hate from growing. Here, children participate in the "Close the Book on Hate" program, sponsored by the Anti-Defamation League.

In 1995 the Public Broadcasting Service televised a documentary about Billings titled *Not In Our Town*. Since then, the documentary has inspired people in hundreds of other communities to band together to fight hate crimes. In Contra Costa County, California, Barbara and Ed Tonningsen formed a Not In Our Town group after they saw the film. When a mosque was vandalized after the September 11, 2001, attacks, group members called Muslims to show their support. NIOT member Susan Hedgpeth says, "That human-to-human connection, that's very powerful, and I think that's how we change things."[98]

Individuals Fight Hate Crimes

Such one-on-one contact is a powerful weapon in fighting hate crimes. Yet there are many other ways people can make a difference in that battle as well. During the 1999 Fourth of July holiday weekend, Benjamin Nathaniel Smith killed two people and wounded nine others during racially motivated drive-by shootings in Illinois and Indiana. Former Northwestern University basketball coach Ricky Byrdsong, an African American, was one of the victims Smith randomly chose. When her husband was shot to death on July 2, Sherialyn Byrdsong said she had a choice to make: "I had to dig deep and ask myself some questions. Would I let this turn me into a hater?"[99] Instead of hating whites because one had killed her husband, Byrdsong decided to fight the hatred that led to his death. In the years since then, she has given many speeches in an effort to educate people about hate crimes and their devastating effects.

H<small>ATE</small> C<small>RIMES</small> H<small>URT</small> M<small>ORE THAN</small> J<small>UST THE</small> V<small>ICTIM</small>

"Teach your children to accept and understand diversity because the consequences of hate hurt the families of the victim. It also hurts the families of the perpetrators. Lives are ended and lives are changed forever."

Judy Shepard on the fifth anniversary of the slaying of her son Matthew, who was gay. Judy Shepard, "Five Years Later, Progress Against Gay Hatred Lags," *USA Today*, October 13, 2003, p. A15.

In 1998 Judy Shepard reacted in the same way after her son Matthew was brutally murdered in Wyoming because he was gay. In countless personal appearances and articles for newspapers and magazines, she has tried to get people to fight the hatred that leads to such crimes even though she knows it is a difficult task. Shepard says, "I'm not naive to think that hate isn't alive and well. We're not born knowing how to do that. If we can learn how to hate, then we can unlearn and replace it with love and respect."[100]

Byrdsong and Shepard are famous because of tragedies that touched them, but ordinary people can also fight hate. Parents are the most important individuals in this battle. Morris Dees helped found the Southern Poverty Law Center. Dees believes that he grew up free of the racism that was strong in his native Alabama because of what he learned from his mother and father. Dees recalls, "My parents treated blacks as equal human beings at a time when my playmates' parents treated them as second-class citizens."[101] The example set forth by his parents allowed Dees to overcome the racist comments and behavior that he heard and saw while growing up.

"A Person Just Like Me"

One of the best ways to stop hatred is to make people realize that the people they think are different from them are really not so different after all. That was why sixteen-year-old student Daisy Bond was willing to participate in the Teen OUT Monologues in Santa Fe, New Mexico, in June 2006. Bond says she and other openly gay and lesbian teenagers spoke about their lives so that nongay people could understand them: "It's kind of humanizing. It shows people 'This is a person just like me and my family.'"[102] Once something like that happens, people who seemed quite different may no longer seem so strange; getting to know people is often a good first step to reduce fear and hatred between groups.

Introduction: The Scope of Hate Crimes

1. Federal Bureau of Investigations, *Hate Crime Statistics 2004*. Washington, DC: U.S. Department of Justice, 2005, p. 10.
2. Quoted in Julia C. Mead, "Four Are Held in Attack on Mexican Immigrants," *New York Times*, June 15, 2006, p. B7.
3. Elie Wiesel, "We Choose Honor," *Parade Magazine*, October 28, 2001, p. 4.

Chapter 1: How People Learn to Hate

4. Quoted in Austin Fenner and Scott Shifrel, "Fat Nick Gets 15 Years," *New York Daily News*, July 18, 2006, p. 7.
5. Sara Bullard, *Teaching Tolerance: Raising Open-Minded, Empathetic Children*. New York: Doubleday, 1996, p. 27.
6. Jack Levin and Gordana Rabrenovic, *Why We Hate*. Amherst, NY: Prometheus, 2004, p. 63.
7. Quoted in Robert J. Sternberg, ed., *The Psychology of Hate*. Washington, DC: American Psychological Association, 2005, p. 52.
8. Robert M. Baird and Stuart E. Rosenbaum, eds., *Bigotry, Prejudice, and Hatred: Definitions, Causes, and Solutions*. Buffalo, NY: Prometheus, 1992, p. 13.
9. Quoted in Bullard, *Teaching Tolerance*, p. 29.
10. Quoted in Public Broadcasting Service, "Not In Our Town." www.pbs.org/niot/about/niot1.html.
11. Quoted in Gregory M. Herek, "The 'Us' and 'Them' of Murder," University of California, Davis. www.psychology.ucdavis.edu/rainbow/html/shepard.html.
12. Quoted in Levin and Rabrenovic, *Why We Hate*, p. 116.
13. Quoted in John Spong, "The Hate Debate," *Texas Monthly*, April 2001, p. 66.
14. Quoted in Anti-Defamation League, "The Consequences of Right-Wing Extremism on the Internet." www.adl.org/internet/extremism_rw/inspiring.asp.
15. Quoted in Southern Poverty Law Center, "Immigration Fervor Fuels Racist Extremism." www.splcenter.org/news/item.jsp?aid=186.

16. Jack Levin and Jack McDevitt, "Hate Crimes," Brudnick Center on Violence and Conflict, Northeastern University. www.vio lence.neu.edu/publication4.html.

Chapter 2: Hate Crimes Based on Race

17. Quoted in *Anchorage Daily News*, "Opinion: Hate Crime," February 26, 2001, p. B4.
18. Quoted in Vanessa Hua, "Hate Crime Trial Nears End," *San Francisco Chronicle*, July 12, 2004, p. B1.
19. Quoted in Dinesh D'Souza, *The End of Racism: Principles for a Multiracial Society*. New York: Free Press, 1995, p. 27.
20. Quoted in John Asbury, "Swastikas, Satanic Symbols Mar Homes," *Riverside (CA) Press-Enterprise*, July 11, 2006, p. B1.
21. Quoted in Mark Babineck, "Dragging Death Haunts Quiet Texas Town," *Los Angeles Times*, June 8, 2003, p. A20.
22. Quoted in Nicole Sweeney, "Hate Case Brings 176-Year Term," *Milwaukee Journal Sentinel*, April 26, 2002, p. B1.
23. Quoted in Natasha Kaye Johnson, "Assault Stirs Bad Memories," *Gallup Independent,* June 12, 2006. www.gallupindependent.com /2006/jun/061206bdmmrs.html.
24. Quoted in Donald Altschiller, ed., *Hate Crimes: A Reference Handbook*. Santa Barbara, CA: ABC-CLIO, 2005, p. 20.
25. Quoted in Lisa Muoz, "L.I. Man Faces Hate Crime in Mall Attack," *New York Daily News*, June 7, 2006, p. 19.
26. Quoted in State of Wisconsin, "*State v. Mitchell* 169 Wis. 2d 153 (1992)." www.wicourts.gov/about/organization/supreme/docs/ famouscases20.pdf.
27. Quoted in John Spano, "Hate Crime Charged in Gang Killing," *Los Angeles Times*, June 29, 2006, p. B5.
28. Quoted in George Will, "The Right to Be a Cross-Burning Moron," *Albany (NY) Times Union*, April 10, 2003, p. A17.
29. Quoted in Hua, "Hate Crime Trial Nears End," p. B1.
30. Quoted in Kate Hawley, "A Message of Tolerance, Peace; Hate Crime Victim's Widow Speaks at Annual Vigil," *Peoria (IL) Journal Star*, April 28, 2006, p. B1.
31. Quoted in Larry Welborn, "Hate Crime Brings 10 Years," *Orange County (CA) Register*, June 24, 2006, p. 1.
32. Quoted in Sweeney, "Hate Case Brings 176-Year Term," p. B1.

Chapter 3: Hate Crimes Based on Religion

33. Quoted in Justin Ellis, "Muslims Urge Respect for Religion After Hate Crime," *Portland (ME) Press Herald*, July 6, 2006, p. A1.
34. Quoted in Sternberg, ed., *The Psychology of Hate*, p. 52.
35. Quoted in Richard Winton, Andrew Blankstein, and Megan

Garvey, "Mel Gibson Charged with Misdemeanor," *Los Angeles Times*, August 2, 2006, p. A1.

36. Quoted in Curt Woodward, "Attack on Center Has Unlikely Hero; Seattle Police Call It a Hate Crime," *Houston Chronicle*, July 30, 2006, p. 3.

37. Quoted in United Nations, "UN Seminar Participants Stress Importance of Tolerance, Understanding, Education in Countering Islamophobia," press release, December 7, 2004. www.un.org/News/Press/docs/2004/hr4801.doc.html.

38. Quoted in American Muslim, "CAIR Calls on DOJ to Probe Incident as Violation of Civil Rights." www.theamericanmuslim.org/tam.php/features/articles/video_shows_bullet_riddled_quran_thrown_at_tennessee_mosque/009756.

39. Quoted in Scott Williams, "Dolan Stirs Crowd at Holy Hill; Archbishop Tries to Heal Outrage After Site's Vandalism," *Milwaukee (WI) Journal Sentinel*, June 11, 2006, p. B1.

40. Quoted in John Ellement, "Everett Church Vandalism Eyed for Possible Scandal Tie," *Boston Globe*, November 2, 2002, p. B1.

41. Quoted in George Joseph, "Idols Vandalized at Minnesota Temple," *India Abroad*, April 21, 2006, p. A1.

42. Quoted in Marshall Allen, "Baptist Church Vandalized," *San Gabriel Valley (CA) Tribune*, March 14, 2006, p. 1.

Chapter 4: Hate Crimes Based on Sexual Orientation

43. Quoted in Natalie Storey, "Gay Man Beaten to Be Scared Straight," *Santa Fe New Mexican*, August 15, 2006, p. C1.

44. Mark Potok, "Rage on the Right," *Intelligence Report*, Winter 2003. www.splcenter.org/intel/intelreport/article.jsp?aid=141.

45. Quoted in Gregory M. Herek, Jeanine C. Cogan, and J. Roy Gillis, "Victim Experiences in Hate Crimes Based on Sexual Orientation," *Journal of Social Issues*, 2002, vol. 58, p. 329.

46. Quoted in John M. Glionna, "Two Guilty of Killing Transgender Teen; the Men Bludgeoned and Choked Gwen Araujo After Accusing Her of Deceiving Them About Her Biological Identification," *Los Angeles Times*, September 13, 2005, p. B1.

47. Quoted in Debra Chasnoff, "How to Stop Hate Crimes," *Advocate*, August 15, 2006. www.advocate.com/exclu sive_detail_ektid35448.asp.

48. Quoted in Steven Elbow, "Four Charged with Hate Crimes," *Madison (WI) Capital Times*, January 18, 2006, p. A10.

49. Quoted in Candace Rondeaux, "Vandalism Damages More than Property; for Gay Couple, Fear Hits Home," *Washington Post*, August 6, 2006, p. T3.

50. Quoted in Herek, Cogan, and Gillis, "Victim Experiences in Hate

Crimes Based on Sexual Orientation," p. 333.

51. Quoted in Celeste Katz, "Teen Sought in Wild Attack at Gay Bar," *New York Daily News*, February 3, 2006, p. 12.

52. Quoted in Bob Moser, "'Disposable People,'" *Intelligence Report*, Winter 2003. www.splcenter.org/intel/intelreport/ article.jsp?aid =149.

53. Quoted in Chris Summer, "The Victims of Prejudice," BBC News Online. www.news.bbc.co.uk/2/hi/americas/3219591.stm.

54. Quoted in Tom Owens, "Every Story Counts: LGBTQ Activists Rally at Capitol," March 8, 2006. www.tolerance.org/news/article _tol.jsp?id=1367.

55. Diana Wess, "Hate Speech Disturbs," *Fort Collins Coloradoan*, June 21, 2006, p. 3.

56. Quoted in 365Gay.com, "Hate Crimes Against Gays," August 9, 2006. www.365gay.com/Newscon06/08/080906 hate.html.

Chapter 5: Hating Immigrants, the Disabled, and the Homeless

57. Quoted in Nate Carlisle, "Latino Student: Attackers Flung Fists and Racist Words," *Salt Lake Tribune*, May 1, 2006, p. 1.

58. Quoted in Southern Poverty Law Center, "Immigration Fervor Fuels Racist Extremism."

59. Quoted in Southern Poverty Law Center, "Immigration Fervor Fuels Racist Extremism."

60. Quoted in Troy Anderson, "Migrant Debate Spurs Hate," *Whittier (CA) Daily News*, June 5, 2006, p. 8.

61. Quoted in Southern Poverty Law Center, "Immigration Fervor Fuels Racist Extremism."

62. Quoted in *Arab American View*, "Arson Hits Arab Church," November 5, 2001, p. 1.

63. Quoted in Erica Hall, "Local Arab-Americans Face Uphill Battle Against Public Perception," *King County (WA) Journal*, August 24, 2006, p. 1.

64. Quoted in Raj Jayadev, "Sikh Cab Drivers Say Racism, Recession Put Them in the Crosshairs," *Pacific News Service*, October 27, 2003. www.news.pacificnews.org/news/view_article.html.

65. Kathi Wolfe, "Bashing the Disabled: The New Hate Crime," *Progressive*, November 1995, p. 7.

66. Quoted in Laura Hershey, "Researcher Uses Knowledge to Fight Hate: An Interview with Mark Sherry," *Disability World*, June–August 2003. www.disabilityworld.org/06-08_03/gov/ sherry.shtml.

67. Quoted in All Walks of Life, "Increased Vulnerability to Dangers." www.awoltexas.org/dangers.html.

68. Quoted in Hershey, "Researcher Uses Knowledge to Fight Hate."

69. Quoted in Wolfe, "Bashing the Disabled," p. 7.

70. Quoted in Hershey, "Researcher Uses Knowledge to Fight Hate."

71. Quoted in Laurel J. Sweet, "Homeless Man Set on Fire," *Boston Herald*, March 6, 2006, p. 7.

72. Quoted in Sweet, "Homeless Man Set on Fire," p. 7.

73. Quoted in Laura Crimaldi, "Taped Beating of Homeless Man Triggers Hate-Crime Debate," *Boston Herald*, March 5, 2006, p. 5.

Chapter 6: The Perpetrators of Hate Crimes

74. Quoted in *Memphis Commercial Appeal*, "Suspect in Dragging Saw Racial Killing as Initiation, Felon Says," February 19, 1999, p. A2.

75. Quoted in *Beaumont (TX) Enterprise*, "Personal Web Sites Offer Glimpse of Shattered Lives," February 13, 2006, p. A6.

76. Anti-Defamation League, "Extremism in America: Creativity Movement." www.adl.org/Learn/ext_us/WCOTC.asp.

77. Mark Potok, "Internet Hate and the Law," *Intelligence Report*, Winter 2000. www.splcenter.org/intel/intelreport/article.jsp?aid=288&.

78. Quoted in Chip Berlet, "The Hard Edge of Hatred," *Nation*, August 15, 2006. www.thenation.com/doc/20060828/new_nativism.

79. Quoted in Carolyne Zinko, Stacy Finz, and Julie N. Lynem, "Firebomb Attempt at San Jose Judge's Home; 3 Teenage Suspects Arrested in Alleged Hate Crime," *San Francisco Chronicle*, August 31, 1999, p. A17.

80. Quoted in Ryan Menard, "Teens Seeking a Thrill," *Quincy (ME) Patriot Ledger*, March 6, 2006, p. 1.

81. Quoted in Bob Moser, "Age of Rage: Young Extremists Find New Targets—and New Recruits," *Intelligence Report*, Summer 2004. www.splcenter.org/intel/intelreport/article. jsp?aid=468.

82. Quoted in Rick Lyman, "Three Students Held in Church Fires Set in Alabama," *New York Times*, March 9, 2006, p. A1.

83. Quoted in *Filipino Reporter*, "Filipino Gay Abused by Cops," October 7–13, 2005, p. 1.

84. Quoted in *Filipino Reporter,* "Filipino Gay Abused by Cops," p. 1.

85. Quoted in Rachel La Corte, "Black Man Beaten by New Orleans Police for Public Intoxication Says, 'I Haven't Had a Drink in 25 Years,'" *Cincinnati Herald*, October 11, 2005, p. 15.

86. Quoted in Martha Stoddard, "Trooper with KKK Link Is Back: His Due Process Rights and Contract Were Violated When He Was Fired, His Union Rep Says," *Omaha World-Herald*, August 27, 2006, p. B1.

87. Quoted in Sign On San Diego, "Sanders to Gay-Bashers: 'You Are Cowards,'" July 31, 2006. www.signonsandiego.com/news/metro/20060731-1532-hatecrime.html.

88. Quoted in Geoffrey Fattah, "Three Charged with Hate Crimes," *Salt Lake City Deseret Morning News*, November 4, 2005, p. B1.

Chapter 7: Fighting Hate Crimes

89. Quoted in Joe Mahoney, "Hate Symbols a Crime—Gov," *New York Daily News*, June 16, 2006, p. 35.

90. Quoted in Venice Buhain and Adam Wilson, "Neo-Nazis Speak into Sea of Opponents," *Olympian*, July 4, 2006, p. 1.

91. Karen Zielinski, "Fighting Crime: Commonsense Strategies for Protecting Ourselves," National Multiple Sclerosis Society. www.nationalmssociety.org/IMSSp02-FightingCrime. asp.

92. Quoted in Fenner and Shifrel, "Fat Nick Gets 15 Years," p. 7.

93. Quoted in Anti-Defamation League, "How to Combat Bias and Hate Crimes: An ADL Blueprint for Action," 1999. www.adl.org/99hatecrime.

94. Quoted in Nancy Bartley, "An Act of Hate Brings Faiths Together," *Seattle Times*, August 1, 2006, p. A1.

95. Quoted in Bartley, "An Act of Hate Brings Faiths Together," p. A1.

96. Chasnoff, "How to Stop Hate Crimes."

97. Quoted in Public Broadcasting Service, "Not In Our Town." www.pbs.org/niot/about/niot1.html.

98. Quoted in KQED, "Not In Our Town, Northern California: Citizens Take Action." www.kqed.org/programs/tv/niot/coco.jsp.

99. Quoted in Hawley, "A Message of Tolerance, Peace," p. B1.

100. Quoted in Mike Cassego, "Remembering Matthew Shepard," *York (PA) Daily Record*, April 9, 2004, p. 1.

101. Quoted in Bullard, *Teaching Tolerance*, p. xix.

102. Quoted in Teresa Baca, "Monologues Give Insight to Teens Who Are 'Out,'" *Santa Fe New Mexican*, June 9, 2006, p. D3.

DISCUSSION QUESTIONS

Chapter 1: How People Learn to Hate

1. Why did Nicholas Minucci hate Glenn Moore?
2. How do stereotypes make it easier for people to hate other people?
3. Is the hatred some people feel for people who are different caused by fear?

Chapter 2: Hate Crimes Based on Race

1. Why do many whites feel justified in committing hate crimes against blacks or Asians?
2. Which racial group in the United States has been subjected to more hate crimes than any other?
3. How do historical events like the Vietnam War make some people hate other people?

Chapter 3: Hate Crimes Based on Religion

1. Why do followers of one religion sometimes hate those from another religion?
2. Name some religious groups that are targeted for hate crimes. Who hates them?
3. Why do some people hate Muslims? Is it fair to blame American Muslims for actions by Muslims thousands of miles away?

Chapter 4: Hate Crimes Based on Sexual Orientation

1. Which group of people targeted for hate crimes does Mark Potok of the Southern Poverty Law Center believe is hated more than any other?
2. Why are many sexual-orientation hate crimes never reported?
3. Are hate crimes a big problem in schools?

Chapter 5: Hating Immigrants, the Disabled, and the Homeless

1. Why did many people in the early twenty-first century hate Mexicans?
2. Why would a hate-crime perpetrator mistake a Sikh for a Muslim?
3. Should violent acts against homeless people be considered hate crimes even though government officials do not classify them as such?

Chapter 6: The Perpetrators of Hate Crimes

1. Which is the oldest U.S. hate group? Is it still active in promoting hatred and committing hate crimes?
2. Do most people who commit hate crimes belong to hate groups?
3. What is a neo-Nazi? Are neo-Nazis a powerful hate-crime group?

Chapter 7: Fighting Hate Crimes

1. How do hate-crime laws curb hate crimes?
2. What part do groups play in fighting hate crime?
3. What can individual people do to stop hate crimes?

ORGANIZATIONS TO CONTACT

All Walks of Life
9106 Benthos
Houston, TX 77083
www.awol-texas.org
This group is dedicated to protecting people with disabilities from hate crimes.

American-Arab Anti-Discrimination Committee
4201 Connecticut Ave. NW, #300
Washington, DC 20008
(202) 244-2990
www.adc.org
This group fights discrimination and hate crimes against Arab Americans.

American Association of People with Disabilities
1629 K St. NW, Suite 503
Washington, DC 20006
(800) 840-8844
www.aapd-dc.org/
This national association helps people cope with disabilities and fight discrimination and hate crimes.

Anti-Defamation League
823 United Nations Plaza
New York, NY 10017
(212) 490-2525
www.adl.org
One of the oldest groups in the United States that fights discrimination, the league battles anti-Semitism through educational and legal efforts.

Asian American Legal Defense and Education Fund
99 Hudson St., 12th Fl.
New York, NY 10013-2869
(212) 966-5932 • fax: (212) 966-4303
The fund protects the rights of Asian Americans and educates the public about Asians to prevent discrimination.

Council on American-Islamic Relations

453 New Jersey Ave. SE
Washington, DC 20003-4034
(202) 488-8787 • fax: (202) 488-0833
www.cair-net.org
CAIR works to protect the rights of American Muslims and educate the public about Islam, the Muslim religion.

Human Rights Campaign

1640 Rhode Island Ave. NW
Washington, DC 20036-3278
(202) 628-4160 • fax: (202) 347-5323
www.hrc.org
The Human Rights Campaign is the nation's largest civil rights organization working for gay, lesbian, bisexual, and transgender equality.

National Association for the Advancement of Colored People

NAACP National Headquarters
4805 Mt. Hope Dr.
Baltimore, MD 21215
(877) NAACP-98
www.naacp.org
The NAACP, a predominantly African American organization, has been leading the fight for black civil rights and to end discrimination since 1909.

National Coalition for the Homeless

2201 P St. NW
Washington, DC 20037
(202) 462-4822 • fax: (202) 562-4823
www.nationalhomeless.org.
The group protects homeless people from discrimination and hate crimes.

National Gay and Lesbian Task Force

1325 Massachusetts Ave. NW, Suite 600
Washington, DC 20005
(202) 393-5177 • fax: (202) 393-2241
www.thetaskforce.org
This organization has led the way in the fight for equality for gays and lesbians.

The National Youth Violence Prevention Resource Center

PO Box 10809
Rockville, MD 20849-0809
(866) SAFEYOUTH (723-3968) • fax: (301) 562-1001

www.safeyouth.org
The center works to prevent violence to young people, especially those who are targets of hate crimes.

Parents, Families, and Friends of Lesbians and Gays
1726 M St. NW, Suite 400
Washington, DC 20036
(202) 467-8180 • fax: (202) 467-8194
www.pflag.org
This group supports lesbians and gays in fighting discrimination and denial of their civil rights.

Partners Against Hate
1100 Connecticut Ave. NW, Suite # 1020
Washington, DC 20036
(202) 452-8310 • fax: (202) 296-2371
www.partnersagainsthate.org
Partners Against Hate is a collective effort of the Anti-Defamation League, the Leadership Conference Education Fund, and the Center for the Prevention of Hate Violence.

Southern Poverty Law Center
PO Box 548
Montgomery, AL 36101
(334) 956-8200
www.splcenter.org
This law center was founded in 1971 to combat hate crimes and discrimination against southern blacks. Today it fights hate crimes and discrimination against all types of people.

Books

Annie S. Barnes, *Everyday Racism: A Book for All Americans*. Naperville, IL: Sourcebooks, 2000. Details various types of racism, including hate crimes that people encounter at school, at the workplace, and in public places.

Tahar Ben Jelloun, *Racism Explained to My Daughter*. New York: New Press, 1999. Ben Jelloun and several other people tell how they have explained racism to their children.

Michael Bochenek and A. Widney Brown, *Hatred in the Hallways: Violence and Discrimination Aagainst Lesbian, Gay, Bisexual, and Transgender Students in U.S. Schools*. New York: Human Rights Watch, 2001. Explains hateful acts in schools based on gender identification.

Laura D'Angelo, *Hate Crimes*. Philadelphia: Chelsea House, 1991. A solid overview of hate crimes.

Roman Espejo, ed., *What Is a Hate Crime?* San Diego, CA: Greenhaven, 2002. A collection of articles on all aspects of hate crimes.

Barbara Perry, *In the Name of Hate: Understanding Hate Crimes*. New York: Routledge, 2001. A thorough examination of the issues related to hate crimes.

Tamara L. Roleff, ed., *Current Controversies: Hate Crimes*. San Diego, CA: Greenhaven, 2001. A collection of articles presenting different viewpoints both pro and con on hate crime, their effects on victims, and hate groups.

Caryl Stern-LaRosa and Ellen Hofheimer Bettmann, *The Anti-Defamation League's Hate Hurts: How Children Learn and Unlearn Prejudice*. New York: Scholastic, 2000. This book explores ways to keep children from becoming hateful and has advice on how to cope with hate.

Films

"Not In Our Town." VHS. Oakland, CA: Working Group, 1995. VHS, 30 minutes. Release date: July 30, 1995. Not In Our Town Working Group. This film tells how residents of Billings, Montana, joined together to fight hate when their neighbors were threatened by white supremacists.

"Not In Our Town, II." VHS. Oakland, CA: Working Group, 1997. VHS, 57 minutes. Release date: December 13, 1997. Not In Our Town Working Group. This work briefly recaps the efforts in Billings, Montana, to fight hate crimes and tells six new stories about people working to create hate-free towns, cities, workplaces, and schools.

Web Sites

All Walks of Life . (www.awol-texas.org). This Web site's focus is to prevent violence to people with disabilities.

American-Arab Anti-Discrimination Committee (www.adc.org). A Web site about discrimination and hate crimes against Arabs.

Anti-Defamation League (www.adl.org). This comprehensive Web site has information on all aspects of hate crimes.

Brudnick Center on Violence and Conflict (www.violence.neu. edu). The center, part of Northeastern University, has information on hate crimes and how to curb hatred based on group differences.

LAMBDA (www.lambda.org). This Web site has detailed information on how to prevent, report, and survive hate crimes against gay, lesbian, bisexual, and transgender people.

National Coalition for the Homeless (www.nationalhomeless.org). The coalition provides stories, data, and information on violence against the homeless.

National Youth Violence Prevention Resource Center (www.safe youth.org). This Web site, sponsored by the Centers for Disease Control and Prevention and other federal agencies, has information on how young people can prevent hate crimes.

Parents, Family, and Friends of Lesbians and Gays (www.pflag.org). This organization supports friends and family of gay people.

Partners Against Hate (www.partnersagainsthate.org). A national coalition of several groups that fight all types of hate crimes. Member groups include the Anti-Defamation League, the Leadership Conference Education Fund, and the Center for the Prevention of Hate Violence.

Southern Poverty Law Center (www.splcenter.org). The center has a wealth of information regarding hate crimes, hate groups, and how to prevent hate crimes.

INDEX

PICTURE CREDITS

Cover photo: © Howard Davies/Corbis

AP Images, 7, 9, 11, 16, 18, 20, 22, 26, 27, 32, 36, 37, 39, 42, 45, 48, 53, 55, 63, 66, 68, 71, 72, 75, 78, 79, 81, 83, 84, 87, 88

© Bettmann/Corbis, 29

© Erik Freeland/Saba/Corbis, 61

The Gale Group, 41

Frazer Harrison/Getty Images, 91

The Library of Congress, 24

© Zayra Morales/EFE/epa/Corbis, 59

© Ed Quinn/Corbis, 56

© Reuters/Corbis, 43

© Ariel Skelly/Corbis, 13

United States Holocaust Museum Photo Archives, 10

ABOUT THE AUTHOR

Michael V. Uschan has written more than fifty books, including *Life of an American Soldier in Iraq*, for which he won the 2005 Council for Wisconsin Writers Juvenile Nonfiction Award. It was the second time he won the award. Uschan began his career as a writer and editor with United Press International, a wire service that provides stories to newspapers, radio, and television. Journalism is sometimes called "history in a hurry," and Uschan considers writing history books a natural extension of the skills he developed in his many years as a journalist. He and his wife, Barbara, reside in the Milwaukee suburb of Franklin, Wisconsin.